Michael van Straten

Superfoods

from the Garden

grow it, cook it and achieve the best health ever

CICO BOOKS

LONDON NEW YORK

Published in 2011 by CICO Books
An imprint of Ryland Peters & Small Ltd
20–21 Jockey's Fields
London WC1R 4BW

www.cicobooks.com

10 9 8 7 6 5 4 3 2 1

A CIP catalogue record for this book is available from the British Library.

ISBN 978 1 907563 14 0

Printed in China

Editor: Marion Paull
Designer: Jacqui Caulton
Design concept: Roger Hammond
Photography: All photographs by Hervé Roncière, except:
Caroline Arber page 98; Henry Bourne page 82; Martin Brigdale page 35; Johnathan Buckley page 148;
Peter Cassidy pages 97, 108, 120, 164, 165, 172; Jean Cazals page 125; Caroline Hughes pages 12, 15,
16, 76, 78, 96, 109, 117, 139, 151, 153; William Lingwood pages 127, 169; David Merewether pages 17,
19, 20, 21, 32, 43, 54, 58, 59, 68, 69, 77, 112, 113, 116, 147, 149, 154, 155, 156, 157, 160, 161;
William Reavell page 129; Reflex Stock page 73; Claire Richardson page 34; Heini Schneebeli page 79;
Pia Tryde page 159; Polly Wreford page 158.

Superfoods
from the Garden

Contents

Introduction

These days, I find myself saying 'I told you so' all the time, hateful though that is. I shout it at the TV, bellow it at the radio and mutter it under my breath as I read the newspapers. When times are hard, money short and we all face a reduction in our standards of living, the media does little to help with positive advice for a cheaper but better, healthier and greener life. So I find myself shouting even more.

Why? Because all the things I have been saying about the health of both people and the planet since the sixties are finally coming home to roost: food colouring and pesticides that cause ADHD; baby bottles that trigger abnormal sexual development; painkillers that cause stomach bleeds, heart conditions and death; transfats that cause more heart disease than dripping or lard; white bread that's responsible for IBS and diverticulitis; fat, salt and sugar in processed food being linked to heart disease, high blood pressure, strokes and obesity.

These facts are now accepted by the political and medical establishments. NICE (National Institute for Clinical Excellence) has listed food additives that should be removed, asked for transfats to be outlawed and suggested that food manufacturers improve unhealthy products – but it's all too little, too late. Years ago, when Tony Blair was Prime Minister, I told him that he should introduce a 'fat tax' and improve school meals. He did not listen, and how many millions of UK residents have suffered as a consequence, and how many billions of pounds have industry pocketed in the meantime?

So it's up to us to help ourselves by thinking carefully about what we eat and trying to live more organically. If you want to eat better for less by growing your own, boost your immunity to disease and infection by consuming more nutrient-rich food, give your children the lifetime skills of simple gardening and cooking, you'll find help and advice in this book. Whether you're fortunate enough to have a large garden, or you have a tiny patio, a window box or even a few sunny windowsills, you can grow something edible and delicious. Start with a few salad leaves, and the next step may take you into a whole world of growing your own.

It is not as difficult as you may think to establish a Superfood garden, and to make it as organic as possible. Once you start to compost, you become much more aware of the natural cycle of growing, harvesting and returning the residues to the soil. You don't need to turn green overnight, and it is hugely better to eat non-organically grown fruit and vegetables than no fruit and vegetables. I have encountered parents who have become 'chemophobes' and bring me their sickly children. They are so anxious about chemical residues in fresh food that they would rather the kids went without if they can't find organic produce. That is madness.

Good food and good health go hand in hand, and if in the process of cultivating both, you can do your bit towards reducing our carbon footprint and helping to slow down global warming, that's even better. Without becoming obsessive, every bottle you recycle, every drop of water you reuse, every mile less you travel in the car are small steps in the right direction. The biggest is bringing up your children to have a care for their planet. By fostering this caring attitude in our young, there is more chance that we will, with the combined efforts of millions, make that giant leap for mankind that allows us to pass on a greener and pleasanter world from generation to generation.

An old Edmundo Ros song says, 'If there's anything you like, you can be certain that it's illegal, it's immoral or it makes you fat', but that is not always true. Little in life can bring more pleasure than sharing great food, a glass of good wine, real bread and time with family and friends – and these pleasures mean better health.

Michael van Straten

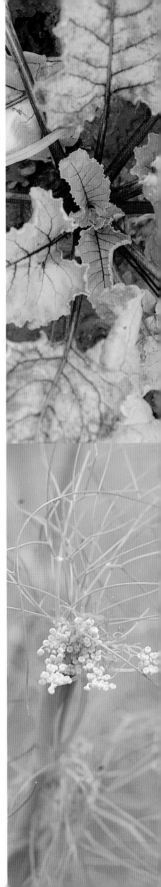

chapter 1
brassicas

cabbage • kale • cauliflower • broccoli
Brussels sprouts • oriental brassicas

Cabbage

Throughout Europe, since the Middle Ages, cabbage has been known as the medicine of the poor, and across the Continent, imaginative cooks have come up with endless ways of eating this amazing member of the brassica family. All brassicas are fairly slow-growing, and cabbages may well take up more room in your garden than most of the other produce.

Cabbage, a source of essential nutrients, has extraordinary healing and health-promoting properties. The dark green leaves contain both iron and the vitamin C necessary for the absorption of this essential mineral. It's also an excellent source of folic acid, which helps prevent birth defects, and contains an abundance of betacarotene, important for the eyes, skin and natural resistance to disease. In populations where large amounts of cabbage are eaten, there is a lower incidence of cancers, especially of the lung, colon, breast and uterus.

Cultivation

Cabbage is one vegetable that you cannot grow in the same place year after year because disease is more likely to develop among your produce. It must be part of your normal crop rotation.

> **SPLENDID SAUERKRAUT**
>
> If, like me, you're a lover of sauerkraut, which is made from shredded and pickled cabbage, you'll be happy to know that it contains billions of protective, gut-friendly bacteria and also a group of cancer-fighting chemicals.

A warm, bruised cabbage leaf wrapped round an inflamed joint relieves the pain. Lining a bra cup, it reduces the pain, inflammation and swelling of mastitis.

All the brassicas need plenty of lime in the soil, with a pH of around 7, to avoid the most common pests and problems. Cabbages are all top-heavy plants and so need firm soil that has been enriched with plenty of organic material at least three months before planting.

Established plants are readily available but you get a much wider choice of varieties by growing from seed. To harvest throughout the winter, sow in late spring and plant out in midsummer. Great varieties are January King, Savoy King and Red Drumhead. For spring cabbage, plant the seed in late summer in the south of England and other warmer areas, in late spring to early summer in northern regions, and plant out early in the autumn.

Wheeler's Imperial is a great old variety, if you can find the seed (try one of the Heritage collections or the Soil Association). It's quite a small cabbage, so withstands winter winds, and has a tight, pointed head, which protects the heart from all but the severest of frosts. Durham Early and Spring Hero are good alternatives.

For summer cabbage, which you can harvest right through until early autumn, plant in late winter or early spring, depending on whether you're in the north

WHY EAT CABBAGE?

VITAMINS K AND C A fantastic source of both with well over half a day's worth from a portion.
FIBRE, MANGANESE AND FOLIC ACID A good source of all three.
IRON This is found in the dark green leafy cabbages and is well absorbed thanks to the vitamin C.
PHYTOCHEMICALS These protective plant chemicals, especially glucosinolates, are abundant in cabbage and account for the cancer-protective properties.

HARVESTING AND STORING

With careful choices, you can be eating your own cabbage all year round. Some varieties will stand well into the winter frosts and hardy Dutch winter varieties will also store for months. Leave some stalk on the head, and hang in nets in a frost-free shed.

Large-leafed and pointed cabbages can be kept in closed bags in the fridge for up to two weeks. Once cut, a cabbage starts to lose vitamin C and some phytochemicals, so seal the cut surface with kitchen film.

HOW TO COOK

Steam, stir-fry, sauté or just wilt young leaves in the water they were washed in. Overcooking causes major nutrient losses so cook for as short a time as possible, in a covered pan where applicable. Cabbage has been shown to lose some of its anti-cancer chemicals after microwaving. (I'm not a fan of the microwave!)

or south of Britain or in a temperate, warm region. You'll need a heated propagator to germinate the seed, and make sure you harden off the plants before putting them out in the garden in mid- to late spring. Derby Day, Summer Monarch and Spitfire are some of the best of British varieties. For autumn cabbage, sow summer cabbage varieties in mid- to late spring, and plant in situ in early summer. These will keep you going until the winter cabbages are ready.

Kale

For decades, kale has been part of the traditional winter diet in Ireland, where it is mixed with mashed potato to make colcannon, which is probably where kale got its name. The Dutch use it in their winter dish stumpot, and the hardy Scots make one of their amazing winter soups, kale brose, with beef, stock, kale and oatmeal.

Kale is one of the hardiest of all the brassicas – most will stand temperatures as low as -15°C, and taste even better after snow or a hard frost. Happily, kale seems to be making a comeback thanks to some fashionable chefs.

There are many varieties available, from dwarf to the giant tree cabbage, or Jersey kale, which can grow to 3.7 metres (12ft) tall on the Channel Islands and in the Vendée region of France. Green, black or red, curly or smooth of leaf, all varieties are fantastically healthy, very low in fat, salt and cholesterol, and strongly anti-inflammatory. Nutritionally, kale comes top of the class.

Kale has particularly attractive leaves so, if you've run out of space in your vegetable beds, it's a great crop to grow alongside flowers.

Surprisingly, animal studies have shown that the cabbage family, including kale, can have a mildly protective effect against radiation. Anyone working with VDU screens – and, in this day and age, what child doesn't spend a great deal of time in front of a computer – or having radiation treatment or lots of X-rays should make sure they eat plenty of lightly cooked kale and raw cabbage. Kale also contains healing and protective mucilaginous

Grow a mixture of kales for different colours and sizes. Protect the larger ones from wind damage by tying to firm stakes.

substances similar to those produced by the mucous membrane of the gut and stomach.

Cultivation

Sow kale seeds in late spring and plant them out in summer. They need very firm planting to withstand winter winds, especially as they can grow to be large plants. If you live in an exposed situation, choose dwarf varieties, which are less affected by winds and can be protected by a covering of snow.

For several years I've grown an Italian variety, which one of my patients brought from her home in Tuscany. It's called Cavolo Nero and produces wonderful clumps of green-black crinkly leaves. This, like many kales, is a perennial and can be left where it is so that by the second or third year of growth it's really prolific and enormous.

It is best to pick the leaves when they are still young because older leaves can become tough with a bitter taste.

WHY EAT KALE?

VITAMINS K, A AND C An excellent source of all these vitamins. One portion provides well over the recommended daily allowance of all three.
FIBRE AND B VITAMINS Good source.
LUTEIN A very rich source of lutein, which is a carotenoid that specifically helps prevent the eye disease age-related macular degeneration (AMD), the most common cause of vision loss in older people.
GLUCOSINOLATES AND OTHER PHYTOCHEMICALS Kale is full of these substances, which provide remarkable protection against many forms of cancer.

HARVESTING AND STORING

Pick leaves from the top throughout the winter. Then, in early spring, small side shoots will sprout from the main stem to provide the earliest cabbage family leaves for your kitchen.

The best way to store all the kales is in the ground. Once you've picked the leaves, they start to lose vitamin C and quickly become limp and unappetizing. They'll keep for a day or two in a slatted wooden box covered with wet newspaper in an airy, frost-free garage or shed.

HOW TO COOK

Most nutrients are preserved by steaming but if you must boil kale, use the minimum amount of water and very little, if any, salt. Save the cooking water to use in soups, stocks or gravies. Young kale is excellent eaten raw in salads.

Kale is much less bitter than dark green, leafy cabbage or spring greens, so it's the perfect vegetable to encourage children to develop a taste for the cabbage family.

Cauliflower

For me, cauliflower is a prince among vegetables. It probably originated in Cyprus and arrived in Italy in the Middle Ages. Although it's a member of the cabbage family, it's unusual because the bit we eat is the flower, not the leaves. Cauliflowers have a long season – there are varieties that produce heads from early spring through to autumn and even into the winter.

Raw in salads or with dips, cooked and served cold with salad dressing or cooked in milk and butter (as the Irish did in the 1800s), cauliflower always tastes great. When you buy one, use your nose. When really fresh, there's hardly any cabbage smell. If the smell reminds you of horrible school cabbage, it has been around too long – don't buy it. Cauliflowers should be white, unless, of course, you're buying one of the coloured types, and firm.

Although cauliflower doesn't contain chlorophyll, unless you eat some of the tender protective green leaves, it's an exceptionally healthy vegetable. As well as a good supply of vitamins and minerals, it contains the same cancer-fighting chemicals as other brassicas and has virtually no saturated fat or cholesterol.

Cultivation

Cauliflowers need nurturing so use rich compost or a good organic fertilizer. Make sure you rotate the crop each year and grow a mixture of varieties so you don't end up with a glut all at once. Sow the seed in small batches at two-week intervals to ensure a continuous supply.

Sow under glass in late winter or outdoors in a prepared seedbed in mid-spring. Winter varieties can be planted in late spring to

While your cauliflowers are growing, fold the leaves over the heads and use the outer leaves of cut plants to keep the hearts white and protect them from insects.

early summer. They'll withstand the winter and can be cropped from early spring to early summer the following year.

It's important not to let the seedlings grow too high before planting out in firm soil. Leave around 30–60cm (1–2ft) between each plant and also between each row, depending on variety. It's worth covering cauliflowers with fine netting until they're established to keep the aphids away. Like all the brassicas, they can attract cabbage whitefly, caterpillars, slugs and, especially, pigeons. I've found that strings of unwanted CDs twisting in the wind make great bird scarers.

For a summer/autumn crop, try Snowball, which matures mid- to late summer. For early and late crops, All-The-Year-Round is a good choice. Australian Snowcap tolerates mild frost and is ready for Christmas time. If you want to experiment with some of the fashionable mini cauliflowers, try to track down a variety called New Igloo. Plant 15cm (6in) apart and they will crop from late summer right through to midwinter.

For a late winter variety, try Snowbred F1, the earliest to crop – before the spring flowers start to show their heads – or the magnificent Purple Cape, an old, deep purple cauliflower, which tolerates frost and is ready by very early spring.

WHY EAT CAULIFLOWER?

VITAMIN C An average portion provides half your daily needs.

VITAMIN B6 Good source.

FIBRE Good source.

PROTEIN Reasonable source.

FOLIC ACID A valuable source of folic acid, which helps protect against birth defects and heart disease.

GLUCOSINOLATES Rich in these substances, which protect against cancer.

SULPHUR AND SULFORAPHANE Rich in these anti-bacterial compounds. Sulforaphane is a chemical released when the plant is chopped or chewed, stimulating the liver to produce enzymes that kill colon cancer cells. It may even help to prevent the spread of breast cancer cells.

BETACAROTENE AND RIBOFLAVIN Contains small amounts of these nutrients, although they are easily destroyed by cooking.

HARVESTING AND STORING

Cut your cauliflowers with a few of the tender green leaves left on. These provide more betacarotene and vitamin C when cooked. Wrapped in their own leaves and kept cool out of sunlight, cauliflowers last for a few days, perhaps a little longer in the salad drawer of the fridge.

HOW TO COOK

Break into small florets and steam or stir-fry, or boil in slightly salted water for as short a time as possible to preserve the nutrients. Cauliflower florets are even better raw in salads and as crudités.

Most children will eat this vegetable – serve as cauliflower cheese for an extra calcium boost to help build strong bones.

Broccoli

Broccoli is a cultivated variety of the original wild cabbage, but is more like cauliflower. In fact, it's sometimes hard to tell the difference between some varieties of broccoli and cauliflower. The original white- and purple-sprouting broccoli are believed to have come from Italy and were first introduced to the UK and France in the early 1700s.

Like the other brassicas, which are also known as cruciferous vegetables, broccoli is a rich source of natural chemicals that protect the body against cancer. As far back as 1987, a study by the American National Cancer Institute examined seven major population studies, and six of them showed that the more cruciferous vegetables you eat, the lower your chances of developing colon cancer. Ever since the scare about President Reagan's bowel cancer, when the Institute advised a special diet for the president that included plenty of broccoli, it has become ever more popular throughout the US.

There are two main types of broccoli that you can grow: the sprouting varieties that have a collection of separate florets on a long stem, and calabrese, which has one firm head.

Cultivation

Avoid exposed sites for your broccoli, and if your soil isn't well drained, dig in plenty of organic matter and sharp sand.

In good soil, purple-sprouting broccoli will easily grow to 1 metre (39in) tall with the same spread. So leave 60cm (24in) between each plant and each row, and make sure to firm the soil around each one

Young, freshly picked sprouting heads are excellent eaten raw as crudités, with a selection of tasty dips.

with your feet. For added protection, I like to stake each plant and earth up a little as they grow.

In warm areas, sow in spring and plant out in summer. In colder regions, delay sowing until midsummer. This will provide a crop early the following year, continuing right through spring and summer. In mild winters, you could be picking purple-sprouting broccoli through to the following spring. Many regional cultivars are available these days, and, with careful choice, these will provide you with a greatly extended season of successive crops.

Unless you're feeding the whole street, 10 to 12 plants will be enough, plenty for a small family.

For calabrese, sow directly where the plants are to grow in late spring and summer for harvesting in late summer and autumn. Leave 30cm (12in) between each plant and 45cm (18in) between each row.

WHY EAT BROCCOLI?

CAROTENOIDS Present in large quantities, especially betacarotene. The body turns these into vitamin A, and one portion of broccoli gives you half your day's requirement of this nutrient, which is essential for fighting cancer and for promoting natural resistance and healthy skin.
VITAMIN C An excellent source, a whole day's dose in one average portion.
FOLATE A good source, 15 per cent of a day's dose in an average portion.
MINERALS A good source of thiamine, niacin, selenium, iron, calcium and magnesium.
PROTEIN Good source.

HARVESTING AND STORING

For purple-sprouting broccoli, pick the shoots before the florets open and take a few from each plant to stimulate new growth. If you denude an entire plant, you'll be lucky if you get any new growth. Cut the main heads of calabrese before they get too big and before the flower buds open. Leave the side shoots for the chance of a second harvest.

A few days in the salad box of your fridge or in a cool, airy garage is the maximum possible storage. Broccoli is at its best and most delicious when you pick it, cook it and eat it within a few hours.

HOW TO COOK

Steam, or boil very gently in lightly salted water until the stalks are tender. It can also be eaten cold in salads.

Brussels sprouts

This member of the brassica family really did originate in gardens near to the Belgian capital. Early records go as far back as the thirteenth century. They are mentioned in the regulations for holding markets in the year 1213 when they were called 'spruyten', or sprouts, so not much has changed in 800 years.

My mother was a wonderful cook. She never used a recipe and hardly ever weighed or measured any ingredients. She cooked with love and instinct and there were always friends and relatives waiting to fill any empty seats at her table – but she could assassinate greens, boiling them half to death. This was such a common practice 50 years ago that generations grew up with an in-built fear and loathing of everything green, especially the sulphurous Brussels sprout.

This is a bad, unfair and undeserved rap. Properly cooked, Brussels are not only tasty but versatile, and one of the richest sources of nature's own cancer-protective chemicals. They supply folic acid, betacarotene (which your body converts to vitamin A), and minerals galore. If you've got space in your garden, they're one of the most rewarding brassicas to grow.

I like the old-fashioned, maincrop varieties, especially Seven Hills. They will happily survive temperatures down to -10°C and taste even better after a bit of frost. I can promise you that the pleasure of eating fresh Brussels sprouts is well worth the frozen fingertips you'll get from picking them on an icy, white Christmas morning.

Sprouts will always taste better after the frost has been on them, so trust me, it really is worth leaving them until then.

Cultivation

You can either buy your plants ready grown or sow seed in a germinator in the early spring. I put mine in 10cm (4in) pots, which leaves enough space for the strong tap roots to develop. Plant them out in late spring to early summer, but remember tall varieties need plenty of room, ideally 70cm (28in) between plants and 90cm (36in) between rows. I always plant a few marigold plants along the row to keep away the whitefly, and there's plenty of room to plant radishes or a selection of cut-and-come-again salad crops between the rows.

About six weeks after planting, draw some surface soil up around the roots to give them extra support. It's very important to stake the tall plants to stop them rocking in the wind, which will loosen and damage the roots. Sprouts on the same stem won't all mature at the same time, so you can pick them continuously from early winter often through to early spring. If you plant the early and late varieties, you can be eating your own home-grown sprouts from late summer to the middle of the following spring.

There's a double bonus with Brussels sprouts – the top leaves can be eaten just like cabbage after the sprouts have all gone.

WHY EAT BRUSSELS SPROUTS?

VITAMINS C AND K Excellent source. A helping of five sprouts provides at least your daily requirement of both.
VITAMINS B2, B6, FOLIC ACID AND BETACAROTENE Very good source.
FIBRE Very good source.
MINERALS A very good source of potassium and manganese.
GLUCOSINOLATES Sprouts have an abundant supply of the most important glucosinolates, glucobrassicin and sinigrin. In response to cell damage, these chemicals are converted into cancer-fighting indoles. In Japan, the average intake of glucosinolates is 100mg a day and the Japanese have an extremely low incidence of colon cancer. In the UK, however, there's a very high incidence of colon cancer and the intake of glucosinolates is less than a quarter of the Japanese consumption. To reduce your risk of colon cancer, eat a portion of sprouts or their relatives at least three times a week.

HARVESTING AND STORING

It's best to take sprouts from the bottom of the stem, working your way up. Use a sharp knife to make a clean cut, and leave a small stump on the stem to encourage the growth of more sprouts later in the season. Pulling them off tears the skin from the stem and prevents new vegetables forming.

Don't remove the Brussels tops until the stems are bare, when you can either take a few leaves at a time or the entire top in one go.

Due to their dense, compact nature, Brussels will store a little better than other members of the cabbage family. Hang them in nets in an airy shed or garage. However, bear in mind that every day that passes after harvesting means a loss of nutrients.

HOW TO COOK

Brussels sprouts can be steamed, lightly boiled, stir-fried or roasted. If you boil or steam them for more than 10 minutes, though, the vegetables will no longer be crunchy, bright green and delicious. They're traditionally served with cooked chestnuts, tossed in butter with a sprinkle of nutmeg.

A popular way of using any leftover cooked Brussels is to make them into a soup with Stilton – a sin, I think – and sprinkle the soup with herbs, such as flat-leaf parsley, tarragon, basil or oregano.

Cook Brussels tops like cabbage (see page 11).

Oriental brassicas

Plants of this family have been grown since man's first efforts at cultivation. The Chinese have grown them for food and medicine since around 3000 BCE, and millennia of cross-pollination of the many varieties have led to the current wonderful range of flavours, textures and growing habits. It may have taken many of us until the twenty-first century to discover the benefits of growing and cooking our own, but now we can enjoy the extraordinary nutritional bonus that they bring to the table.

Oriental brassicas are a great introduction to gardening for kids because they're quick and easy, but they're also a most rewarding crop for the kitchen garden. As well as adding some of them raw to salads, others can go straight from cutting to wok, soup pot or steamer. These are genuine Superfoods that can be grown in even the tiniest garden. I always have a couple of pots right by the kitchen door for a last-minute addition to the pan.

Oriental brassicas are often referred to collectively as Chinese cabbage, Chinese leaves and Chinese greens, although the mustard leaves mizuna and mibuna come from Japan. These distant cousins of the turnip add bite to any salad. Mibuna has a slightly stronger flavour. They're also

Red, variegated varieties have a higher betacarotene content and may be quite peppery in flavour.

both great in stir-fries and make a fine base for soups.

Most oriental brassicas have several different varieties and all are nutrient rich – calcium, vitamin A and iron are found in good amounts in all the different types of pak choi, for instance. One of my favourites is a cut-and-come-again mixture of flavours from mild to hot and sweet to bitter. A combination of the leaves provides a great variety of taste, texture and very important health benefits. All the Chinese leaves are anti-ageing – better for your wrinkles than the most expensive pots of cream – and they help control blood pressure, build strong bones, improve digestion, prevent birth defects, preserve eyesight and help fight asthma, bronchitis and emphysema. As a bonus, thanks to their B6, magnesium and potassium content, they relieve the symptoms of PMS.

Cultivation

Sow the oriental brassicas from seed, and most are ready to use within six weeks. I especially like tatsoi, which has open, dark green, glossy, flat leaves, and Green Rocket, which produces tall cylindrical cabbages. Tatsoi stands well into the winter, and Green Rocket cabbages keep well.

EDIBLE FLOWERS

You may be surprised to learn that many of the other 'greens' used in Asian cooking are not from the cabbage family at all. Japanese greens, chop suey greens and many of the other similar plants are, in fact, edible chrysanthemums. These are also easy to grow from seed and don't need a lot of space.

WHY EAT ORIENTAL BRASSICAS?

BETACAROTENES Rich source of betacarotenes, which are important for skin, lungs and eyesight.
GLUCOSINOLATES These phytochemicals protect against cancer.
VITAMINS A, C AND E Excellent source.
VITAMINS B2 AND 6 Very good source.
FOLIC ACID Good source of folic acid, which is vital for heart health and during pregnancy.
CALCIUM Good source, but not brilliantly absorbed.
FIBRE Good source of valuable fibre.
MINERALS Good source of iron, magnesium and potassium.

HARVESTING

Generally, sow cut-and-come-again varieties of oriental brassicas in the greenhouse or conservatory for a constant supply during the winter. With pak choi, you can pick individual leaves as they mature, cut chunks from the plant, leaving the rest to grow on, or you can pull the whole plant to use the tougher outer leaves in cooking and the tender inner ones raw in salads. I grow Canton Dwarf (a baby variety) and China choy for summer plantings.

Most varieties of pak choi are not very hardy, but they grow well in the greenhouse, conservatory or under cloches. They range from 10cm (4in) up to 46cm (18in) tall.

Pretty well all varieties of mustard leaves can be planted straight into the ground when the soil warms up and so can be sown to produce very early crops. Use an empty wooden fruit box filled with compost or the used growbag from last summer's tomatoes. Sprinkle seed thinly over the box, cover lightly and keep just damp. If using a growbag, cut off the whole top panel and sow three different types of leaves. Again, keep damp but don't overwater. In four to five weeks you could be snipping off wonderful fresh salad leaves.

Mizuna and mibuna grow in bushy clumps and look as good as they taste. Mizuna has dark green, glossy leaves and tender white stalks. Mibuna is more frost-tolerant, with long, slender leaves.

Stuffed cabbage leaves

This is one recipe that really is better with your own home-grown, chemical-free, freshly picked Superfood from the garden – cabbage. Once harvested, the leaves start to lose moisture and become brittle. This makes it much harder to fill, roll and fix the leaves for cooking and eating. If the cabbage leaves have thick stems, cut these out before cooking so you can roll them up more easily when stuffed. The recipe may seem a bit fiddly, but it is easier than it sounds and fabulous to eat. Served with a green salad, this mix of protein and carbohydrate is a perfect balance. Finish the meal with a peach, a handful of grapes and two plums and you've had your five a day.

Serves 4

16 good-sized cabbage leaves

110g (4oz) rice

2 medium onions, chopped

3 tbsp rapeseed oil

350g (12oz) lean minced beef

handful fresh, flat-leaf parsley, washed, dried, chopped

400g (14oz) can chopped tomatoes (peeled and deseeded if using fresh)

Preheat the oven to 210°C/420°F/gas 7.

Plunge the cabbage leaves in boiling, lightly salted water for 5 minutes, drain and set aside to cool.

Cook the rice according to the packet instructions, and drain. Sweat the onions in oil, taking care not to let them brown. Add the rice, meat and parsley, stir and cook for 5 minutes.

Lay 8 of the cabbage leaves separately on a work surface and cover them with the other 8. Spread each pair with the meat mixture and roll into a sausage shape. Oil a deep, ovenproof dish and put in the stuffed cabbage leaves. Drizzle with a little oil and add the tomatoes. Cook in the oven for around 20 minutes.

TIP If you want to avoid the smell of cooking cabbage in the house, bake a thick slice of bread in the oven until crisp. Float one of these giant croûtons on top of the water whenever you boil cabbage.

BENEFITS

■ Contains an enormous amount of chemicals that protect against cancer.

■ Your daily needs of protein, vitamin C, folic acid and lycopene are all wrapped up in these delicious parcels.

Cavalo Nero with red pepper and pancetta

I was given the basics of this dish by our neighbour in England, Vee, who specializes in Spanish cooking. She was inspired by her husband, who spent years working in Spain. It's quick and filling enough to be a light lunch or supper and great as a side dish or cold salad.

BENEFITS

- Cavalo Nero protects against cancer and contains heart-protective nutrients.
- Red peppers provide a huge dose of betacarotene.
- High in natural fibre, this delicious dish improves digestion and helps to lower cholesterol.

Serves 4

2 tbsp olive oil

110g (4oz) chopped pancetta

2 long red peppers, thinly sliced, seeds removed – they're sweeter and thinner skinned than the round variety

500g (18oz) Cavolo Nero leaves, finely shredded

2 tbsp water

2 tsp wholegrain mustard

freshly ground black pepper

Heat the oil in a large pan. Add the chopped pancetta and fry, stirring occasionally, until just crisp. Add the peppers and cook over a gentle heat until just soft.

Meanwhile, simmer the Cavolo Nero in water until just softened – about 4 minutes. Drain, add to the peppers with the water, cover, and cook for another 4 minutes.

Stir in the mustard, season with black pepper (you won't need any salt as the pancetta is quite salty) and serve in a warm bowl.

Sprouts with black pudding, apple and bacon

This is a quick, simple and tasty snack. You can use fresh or frozen sprouts. It's perfect as a supper dish and just as good as a winter afternoon treat sitting by the fire. It combines some of the best of English ingredients in the bacon, black pudding and apple, with a touch of Europe in the brioche. Alternatively, use a thick slice of coarse wholemeal toast. In spite of the fat content, the pros still outweigh the cons.

BENEFITS

- This dish provides more than a whole day's iron in an easily absorbed form.
- It also provides half your daily requirement of folic acid.
- The apple contains fibre, vitamin C and pectin, which helps lower cholesterol.

Serves 4

1 tbsp rapeseed oil

8 slices black pudding

4 rashers organic, English smoked back bacon

8 Brussels sprouts

15g (2½oz) butter

1 large Cox's apple, cored and cut into 8 slices

2 thick slices toasted brioche

Heat the oil in a large pan, add the black pudding and bacon. Fry gently for 5 minutes. Halve the sprouts, add to the pan and fry gently for another 5 minutes.

Melt the butter in another frying pan, add the apple slices and cook over a low heat until they start to soften – 2 or 3 minutes.

Put one slice of the toasted brioche on to each of four warmed plates. Place a rasher of bacon on each brioche and top with 2 slices of black pudding. Arrange the sprouts on one side of the plate and the sautéed apple on the other.

Bombay Brussels sprouts

You don't have to be vegetarian to enjoy this glorious veggie curry. Brussels sprouts team perfectly with chickpeas, and this spicy concoction is a real winner – warming, satisfying and tasting just as good cold the next day. And hidden away in the spices is a treasure-trove of health-giving benefits.

BENEFITS

- This dish contains major nutrients, including protein, vitamin C, betacarotene, fibre and carbohydrates.
- Turmeric protects against stomach cancer.
- Ginger stimulates the circulation.
- Cumin aids digestion.
- Cloves soothe anxieties.
- Garlic fights infections.

Serves 4

1 medium onion, coarsely chopped

1cm (1/2in) fresh ginger, peeled and coarsely chopped

1 clove garlic, coarsely chopped

2 tbsp olive oil

3 cloves

10 peppercorns

1/2 tsp each turmeric, ground cumin and ground coriander

2 x 400g cans organic chickpeas, drained and well rinsed

175g (6oz) Brussels sprouts, parboiled for 3 minutes and refreshed with cold water

400g (14oz) can chopped tomatoes (peeled and deseeded if using fresh)

1 tbsp garam masala

fresh coriander leaves, chopped

Put the onions, ginger and garlic into a food processor and whizz until well combined.

Heat the oil in a large frying pan, add the cloves and peppercorns and heat gently for one minute. Spoon in the onion, ginger and garlic mix and cook gently for 10 minutes, stirring continuously.

Add the turmeric, ground cumin and ground coriander and continue cooking, still stirring, for 2 more minutes.

Add the chickpeas, sprouts and tomatoes and simmer for 10 minutes, adding a little water if necessary. Stir in the garam masala and scatter the chopped coriander leaves over the finished dish to serve.

Greens soup

I adore soup. I remember Sir Paul McCartney telling me that he'd rather have a bowl of his late wife Linda's home-made soup than eat at any posh restaurant. How I agree! This recipe really is a meal in itself – delicate, delicious and substantial. You won't want anything after it except, maybe, a piece of fruit. This amazingly simple soup has the most delicate and intriguing flavour. Avoid all temptations to add rice, pasta, barley or any other thickening, as the texture is already a unique factor in this virtually saturated-fat-free, nourishing and restorative Asian version of the traditional 'Jewish penicillin', chicken soup.

Serves 6

1 large chicken breast

1.5 litres (2 1/2 pints) chicken stock, preferably home-made

1 generous handful young oriental greens, mixed

2 heads pak choi, green parts only

2 tbsp rapeseed oil

2 tbsp sherry

Mince the chicken finely using a hand mincer or food processor. Put the mince into a bowl and pour over just enough chicken stock to cover it. Leave until the rest of the ingredients are ready.

Cook the greens and pak choy until just wilted. Drain well and chop finely. Heat a wok or large frying pan. Add the oil and stir-fry the greens for 30 seconds, stirring constantly.

Pour in the rest of the stock and the sherry. Add the chicken mixture and bring to a boil. Simmer for 10 minutes.

BENEFITS

- Overflows with protein, folic acid, B vitamins and a vast supply of heart-nourishing and immune-boosting nutrients that also protect against cancer.

Filo cauliflower tart with red onion and maple syrup

It may sound bizarre to add maple syrup to cauliflower, onion and goat's cheese, but this recipe is very tasty. It's from my French neighbour's daughter. She lives in Canada and fuses traditional French cooking with the flavours of her New World.

BENEFITS

- Cauliflower is rich in glucosalinates and sulforaphane, which protect against cancer.
- Cauliflower also contains antibacterial sulphur compounds.
- Onions contain fibre, vitamin C, vitamin B6, potassium and heart-protective chemicals.

Serves 4

400g (14oz) cauliflower, trimmed and cut into small florets

4 sheets ready-made filo pastry

extra virgin olive oil

4 flat, round goat's cheeses

2 red onions, thinly sliced

salt and freshly ground black pepper

60ml (4 tbsp) maple syrup

Preheat the oven to 220°C/425°F/gas 7.

Cook the cauliflower in salted, boiling water for 10 minutes, drain and cool a little.

Lay the filo sheets on a worksurface and brush each one with a little olive oil. Place in a deep baking dish (23cm/9in in diameter) on top of each other, placing each sheet at a different angle. Then trim the edges.

Cut the cheeses into thin, round slices and cover the pastry with them. Sprinkle with half the onions. Cover with the cauliflower, add the rest of the onions and season. Drizzle the maple syrup over the top.

Bake in the oven for 15 minutes or until the tart starts to brown on top.

Beef and brassica stir-fry with sesame seeds

The trick whenever you cook a stir-fry is to prepare all your ingredients beforehand. Recipes sometimes take longer to read than to do, so please don't let the extensive list of ingredients and number of steps put you off. Once you have made a few, it is really fast and furious. High temperatures and superfast cooking mean very little of the oil is absorbed by the food – unlike in all deep-frying – and nutrient losses are minimized. Using rice noodles means there is no gluten, but those with an allergy or coeliac disease should take care because soy sauce usually contains some gluten.

BENEFITS

■ This is a high protein, anti-cancer, heart-protective and cholesterol-lowering dish.

Serves 4

1 packet Chinese rice noodles

3 tbsp peanut oil

2 large onions, chopped

2 cloves garlic, finely chopped

2 small turnips, cubed

2 tsp coriander seeds

2 tbsp sesame seeds

½ tsp paprika

1 head broccoli, cut into small florets

¼ head cauliflower, cut into small florets

600g (1¼lb) fillet steak, cut in thin slices

2 tbsp runny honey

2 tbsp soy sauce

Cook the noodles according to the packet instructions, drain and set aside. Heat your wok, or very large frying pan, and add the oil. Add the onions, garlic, turnips, coriander seeds, half the sesame seeds and the paprika. On high heat, stir briskly for 1 minute. Add the broccoli and cauliflower, and cook, stirring, for 5 minutes. Add the beef and do not stop stirring for another 5 minutes. Then transfer the beef mixture to a hot dish.

Add the honey and soy sauce to the wok and simmer for 60 seconds. Put the beef mixture back in briefly, stir and then transfer all the contents of the wok to the hot dish and cover.

Add a little more oil to the wok, then the noodles, and stir constantly for 90 seconds. Put the noodles on warm plates, top with the beef mixture, and sprinkle on the rest of the sesame seeds to serve.

Garlic beans and pak choi

Canned beans are a godsend. They're quick to prepare, inexpensive and last in the store cupboard for ages – just the thing to form the basis of a nutritious meal when you get home late from work or friends pop in unexpectedly. The combination of beans and greens is health on a plate.

Serves 2 (or 4 as a starter)

90ml (6 tbsp) olive oil

2 cloves garlic, finely chopped

400g (14oz) can cannellini beans, drained and well rinsed

2 heads pak choi, sliced lengthwise

Heat half the oil and all the garlic in a saucepan, but don't allow to brown. Add the beans and heat through, stirring constantly. When hot, mash coarsely with a fork or potato masher. Cover and keep warm.

Heat the remaining oil in a wok and stir-fry the pak choi for 3 minutes, stirring constantly.

Arrange the beans on the plates and top with the pak choi.

BENEFITS

- Containing fibre, protein, vitamins, minerals and plant hormones, this quick and easy dish does more for your health than a constellation of Michelin stars.
- The special soluble fibre in all the legumes helps the body get rid of cholesterol and so protects the heart and circulatory system.

Mongolian hotpot

I make this in a traditional Chinese or Mongolian pot, which is like a fondue pan but with a chimney and a night light that keeps it hot. Any cast-iron or ovenproof dish is fine, though, so long as you can put it on a hot plate in the middle of the table. The idea is to pick out your mouthful from the communal pot and dip it in your own dish of sauce before eating. This is called 'shabu-shabu' in the Far East, which means 'swish swish' – the noise made as you move the meat or vegetable around with your chopsticks in the hot broth. This dish is not only fun and delicious, it's also very nutritious and healthy.

Daikon, a large white Japanese radish, has a distinctive flavour, but ordinary radishes, mouli or a small quantity of horseradish are all good alternatives.

Serves 6

1.5 litres (2 1/2 pints) vegetable or chicken stock, preferably home-made

600g (1 1/4lb) mixed slivers skinless chicken breast, very lean beef steak and small cubes of tofu

1/2 large Chinese cabbage, shredded

2 handfuls any other Chinese greens, shredded

110g (4oz) mushrooms, sliced

4 spring onions, finely chopped

3 heads pak choi, chopped

juice of 2 lemons

2 tbsp soy sauce

1 tbsp mirin (from supermarkets or Asian grocers)

1 daikon or 6 large radishes, grated

Bring the stock to the boil, add the meat and simmer for 5 minutes. Add the tofu and all the vegetables and continue simmering for another 10 to 15 minutes. Add more stock if required to keep the ingredients covered.

In another pan, mix the lemon juice with the soy sauce. Add 90ml (6 tbsp) of stock from the cooking pot. Stir in the mirin and the grated daikon or radishes. To serve, put the hotpot in the middle of the table and give each guest a small dish of sauce.

BENEFITS

- This dish combines protein, vitamins, minerals and natural enzymes.
- It has very little fat.
- 100g (3½oz) of daikon provides more than a third of your day's vitamin C as well as enzymes that help the digestion of starchy foods.

Sweet and sour sea bream on greens

Sea bream is one of the healthiest of fish. It's full of essential nutrients and very easy to digest. Put it on a bed of vitamin-packed Chinese greens and you have a wonderfully light but sustaining meal. All it needs is a portion of rice as an accompaniment and you have a delightful dinner for two that would be perfect for St Valentine's Day! Kale, Brussels tops or spring greens are good alternatives if you don't have any Chinese greens growing in your gourmet garden.

Serves 2

450g (1lb) Chinese greens

4 spring onions

2.5cm (1in) fresh ginger, finely grated

2 sea bream, filleted

60ml (4 tbsp) light soy sauce

2 tbsp Worcestershire sauce

1 tbsp runny honey

2 cloves garlic, very finely chopped

Trim and discard any tough outer leaves from the Chinese greens and wash the remainder thoroughly. Put them together with the spring onions and ginger into a steamer with several centimetres (or inches) of water in the main pan. Lay the fish on top of the vegetables. Cover and steam for about 10 minutes, until the fish is translucent.

Meanwhile, make the dressing by whisking together the soy sauce, Worcestershire sauce, honey and garlic.

Carefully remove the fish from the steamer. Lay the vegetables on serving plates. Place the fish on top and pour over the dressing.

BENEFITS

■ Sea bream contains iodine, an essential trace element that is hard to find.

■ The greens are full of iron and betacarotene.

■ Garlic has heart-protective nutrients.

■ Fish, ginger, honey, soy and garlic are all traditional aphrodisiacs in the Far East, so don't say I didn't warn you!

Cauliflower soufflé

Don't be frightened or put off by the idea of a soufflé. This one is amazingly easy to make, and delicious – a great starter for six people, or served with salad as a light lunch for four. What's more, it makes you look like a kitchen genius!

Is it remotely possible that a dish that looks this fantastic, tastes amazing and contains eggs, cheese and flour can actually be good for you? Yes, Yes. Yes. Just because it seems a bit 'naughty but nice' does not mean it's death on a plate. Good nutrition is a question of balance and what you eat most of the time. This may be a treat but it abounds in health-promoting nutrients, so enjoy and don't feel guilty.

BENEFITS

- This dish is full of calcium.
- It protects against cancer.

Serves 4 (or 6 as a starter)

1 white cauliflower, very fresh and firm

45g (1½oz) unsalted butter

45g (1½oz or 3 heaped tbsp) plain flour, sieved – it's worth making the effort!

350ml (12fl oz) whole milk

2 large free-range eggs, well beaten

150g (5oz) Emmenthal cheese, grated

freshly ground nutmeg

freshly ground black pepper

35g (1¼oz or 2 heaped tbsp) wholemeal breadcrumbs

Preheat the oven to 200°C/400°F/gas 6.

Remove the core and steam the cauliflower whole until it just begins to soften but still retains its crunchiness. Allow it to dry, then break into small florets.

In a good-sized, thick-bottomed saucepan, heat the butter until it melts and stops frothing. On no account let it turn brown.

Add the flour a spoonful at a time, stirring constantly to make a thick roux. Warm the milk and add a little at a time to the flour and butter mixture, stirring constantly. Don't worry, the lumps will disappear as long as you keep stirring.

When all the milk is added, bring to the boil and keep stirring until the liquid starts to thicken. Remove from the heat, then whisk in the eggs, cheese, nutmeg and pepper.

Butter a soufflé dish, add the cauliflower, then the sauce until the mixture is a centimetre or two (inch or two) from the rim of the dish. Top with the breadcrumbs and put straight into the oven for about 45 minutes. You'll know when it's done because it will rise above the dish's rim and have a golden crusty top. Eat straightaway. A salad of wafer-thin slices of cucumber with a lemon-juice dressing goes perfectly with this dish.

Cauliflower soup with salmon kebabs

What a perfect Sunday brunch, light evening meal or very smart starter this is! It not only looks good and tastes great, but is a genuine Superfood recipe, a veritable pharmacy of good health – simple, inexpensive yet a boost for brains, bones and body.

BENEFITS

- Cauliflower contains cancer-fighting chemicals and folic acid.
- Salmon has omega-3 fatty acids for a healthy heart and active brain.
- Vitamin D and protein also come from the salmon.
- Sesame seeds contain vitamin E.

Serves 4

850ml (1½ pints) water

1 cauliflower, cut into florets

1 bunch chives, finely snipped

2 tbsp fish-stock concentrate

100ml (3½fl oz) reduced-fat cream

2 tbsp sesame seeds

1 free-range egg, beaten

4 salmon steaks, cut into cubes

4 tbsp rapeseed oil

Bring the water to the boil in a large saucepan. Add the cauliflower, chives and half the fish stock, and cook for 15 minutes. Leave to cool a little, then liquidize with the cream, and season to taste.

Mix the sesame seeds with the rest of the fish stock and pour into a shallow dish. Put the beaten egg in another shallow dish.

Thread the salmon cubes onto several wooden skewers. Roll the kebabs in the egg and then in the sesame seeds. Fry for 2 minutes on each side.

Reheat the soup and serve in four bowls with one or two kebabs balanced across the top of each.

'Upside-down cake' of rice, meat and vegetables

Well, it may sound bizarre, but don't mock until you've tried it. This is a genuine 'sorlin' recipe from the pub at the bottom of my garden when we lived in Buckinghamshire. Most days there was a 'sorlin' pie, casserole, soup or, as in this case, surprise on the menu. The unwary stranger would look puzzled and ask what these dishes were. 'It's all in there,' came the reply, describing these wonderful leftovers recipes perfectly. This dish is easy to prepare, especially if the serving bowls are all the same size.

BENEFITS

- This dish is a treasure chest of body-building nutrients that boost the immune system.
- It has significant amounts of nearly all the essential nutrients.

Serves 4

3 tbsp peanut oil

2 small beef steaks and 2 chicken breasts, cut into slivers

2 turnips and 2 carrots, cut into sticks

½ white cabbage, finely chopped

a few red lettuce leaves, shredded

1 large red onion, finely chopped

6 mushrooms, sliced

pinch ground ginger

2 tbsp light soy sauce

600g (1¼lb) cooked rice

4 free-range eggs

4 sprigs fresh coriander, chopped

Heat a large wok and pour in two-thirds of the oil. Brown the meat, then take it out of the wok. Add all the vegetables, the ginger and the remaining oil to the wok and stir-fry for about 10 minutes. Put back the meat and add the soy sauce to heat through.

Oil four bowls and fill to about a third with the mixture. Cover with the rice, tapping it all firmly down.

Fry the eggs and, while they're cooking, cover each bowl with a plate, tip upside down and shake gently to free the contents. Put one egg on top of the mound and serve.

Colcannon with Chinese cabbage and poached eggs

There are many recipes for colcannon, but this is my favourite. It comes from my Irish wife, who also makes the best poached eggs this side of the Irish Sea. Since we started growing oriental brassicas, Sally has been using Chinese cabbage to add her own touch to this traditional dish, which more than makes up in health-giving benefits for a bit of butter and a dash of cream. Sticking your fork in the egg and watching the deep yellow yolk trickle over the potato is half the fun.

BENEFITS

- Provides a whole day's vitamins A and C, masses of vitamin K and a good dose of iron, folic acid and protein.
- The potatoes provide energy, while Chinese cabbage protects against cancer.

Serves 4

1kg (2¼lb) old potatoes, preferably Desiree, peeled and diced

700g (1½lb) Chinese cabbage, finely shredded

2 spring onions, finely chopped

300ml (10fl oz) semi-skimmed milk

2 tbsp double cream

4 free-range eggs

1 tbsp white wine vinegar

50g (2oz) unsalted butter

coarse sea salt and freshly ground black pepper

Steam the potatoes until just cooked. Sprinkle the cabbage with a pinch of sea salt, and steam until tender – about 10 minutes. Put the spring onions in the milk and bring almost to the boil. Mash the potatoes, adding a little of the hot milk and spring-onion mixture at a time until smooth. Add the cream and whisk with a fork. Add the cabbage and some black pepper and mix thoroughly. Turn into a hot dish and keep warm.

Roll the eggs for 1 minute in a large pan of slowly simmering water to which the vinegar has been added. Remove them with a slotted spoon, then break them into the centre of the pan of water and continue to simmer for 4 minutes.

Spoon a mound of colcannon onto each plate, making a hollow in the top. Drop in a knob of butter and carefully add the poached eggs.

chapter 2
onion family

garlic • onions • leeks • chives

Garlic

Essential in classical Greek and Roman cooking, garlic was, and still is, a vital flavour of the Mediterranean, and one of the most valuable of all medicinal plants. Indeed, it was used as currency by the Ancient Egyptians.

For centuries, garlic has been used for the treatment of coughs, colds, chest infections and sinus problems. Herbalists have known since the Middle Ages that it could help with asthma, digestive problems, stomach upsets and fungal infections, so it's not surprising that modern science has proved that garlic has powerful antibacterial and antifungal properties. What is surprising is the link between garlic and heart disease. During the last 30 years, evidence has emerged to show that garlic's natural chemicals help the body to get rid of cholesterol. Eating garlic reduces bad cholesterol in the blood, makes the blood less sticky so it's less likely to clot and even helps to lower blood pressure. It's no coincidence that in the countries where most garlic is eaten, fewer people die of heart attacks than in the UK or America.

FOOT CURE

Garlic was brought to Britain by Roman centurions who wedged fresh cloves between their toes to prevent foot rot. Some of the discarded garlic took root and this wonderful wild plant soon became established. How right the soldiers were! The best cure for athlete's foot is to put two crushed cloves of garlic and two tablespoons of cider vinegar into a bowl of hot water and soak the foot for 15 minutes a day.

Choose carefully

My first efforts at growing garlic were pretty miserable and I ended up with cloves that looked like emaciated spring onions. I'd been saving a few cloves of French or Italian garlic and just pushing them into the soil in the garden. For growing successful crops, the first essential is to choose the right variety for the local climate. For example, Isle of Wight garlic is bred for the UK climate and seasons. In the US, huge garlic festivals are staged, the most famous in Gilroy, California, where the best varieties are on show to 100,000 visitors a year. Make sure you order your bulbs in good time for planting early varieties in the autumn.

Cultivation

Garlic prefers a light, free-draining soil and sunshine but it will grow even on heavy clay soil. It likes potash so I save all the ash from our log fires and bonfires and rake it into the soil before planting. Most varieties do better if they have a couple of months of cold weather – below 10°C. Plant the earliest varieties from mid- to late autumn, and use these first when they mature – they won't store as well as the later ones, which should be planted from midwinter to early spring.

Separate the bulbs into cloves, make a 5cm (2in) deep hole with a dibber and push the clove into the hole flat end down. Plant the cloves 15cm (6in) apart with 30cm (12in) between rows. If your soil is very heavy, put a handful of mixed coarse sand and soil improver at the bottom of each hole. Apart from a bit of weeding and watering if very dry, you can leave garlic to fend for itself.

It's very important to rotate your garlic. Don't plant the cloves in the same place, or where onions have grown, for at least three or four years because they are subject to certain forms of rot. However, they resist and repel most pests, which is why companion planting with lettuce, the cabbage family, beetroot and roses protects these plants, too, making garlic a great crop for the organic gardener.

WHY EAT GARLIC?

ALLICIN An excellent source of this sulphur compound, which helps the body to get rid of bad cholesterol and reduce the amount of unhealthy fats produced by the liver.

VITAMINS AND MINERALS A good source of calcium, selenium, phosphorus, vitamins C and B6, although unless you're going to munch your way through whole heads of garlic, you will get more of these from eating an apple.

ANTIBACTERIAL, ANTI-INFLAMMATORY, ANTIFUNGAL These properties make garlic one of the most widely used medicinal plants in the world.

HOW TO COOK

Garlic is very versatile. It can be chopped or crushed to add to recipes, or roasted whole. If you halve a garlic clove, you'll find a small green part in the middle – it's called the germ. This is best removed as it can be bitter. When cooking onions and garlic together, always start with the onions, as they take longer to cook. Add the garlic after 5 minutes to avoid it being overdone, burnt and unpleasant to eat.

Garlic is often used raw. Cut, squeeze and rub it around a salad bowl, or on bread, or add it to almost any savoury dish.

Its unique flavour can be enjoyed in other ways, too. Many years before Heston Blumenthal began serving his wonderfully quirky and delicious dishes, I was making my own garlic ice cream.

Lifting and storing

As soon as the leaves begin turning yellow, it's time to lift your bulbs, but do it gently because damaged, even bruised, bulbs tend to rot.

It's best to dry garlic in the fresh air, off the ground. In wet weather, put the bulbs under a lean-to roof or in a very airy garage or shed with the windows open. After about a week, I tie them in bunches and hang them from nails in the garage. Rather than risk damage, I tend to leave the dirt on the bulbs until they're used.

Garlic is one of the easiest crops to grow and, with a little practice, you need never buy it for the kitchen again. My stored bulbs easily last until the new crop is ready and usually there are enough left to plant for the next year.

HAND CARE

Some people may develop contact dermatitis after handling large amounts of garlic, but usually this is found only among professional cooks.

Onions

Onions are one of the most satisfying of all the vegetables to grow in your garden. They will keep almost from season to season, look wonderful both growing and hanging in bunches from the shed roof and are a basic ingredient in a huge variety of savoury dishes. In the ancient Middle East, the Egyptians and Jews grew this versatile plant, and in 173 BCE there was even a Jewish town called Onion near the Gulf of Suez.

All members of the onion family are effective destroyers of bacterial and fungal infections, and onions themselves are diuretic (they increase the output of urine). They also help to dissolve and eliminate urea, which is what makes them useful in the relief of rheumatism, arthritis and gout. Recent research in Switzerland shows that onions decrease the rate of bone loss, so eating them might help protect older people, especially women, against osteoporosis. They're very low in calories, around 30 in an average portion, fat-free and provide fibre as well as heart-protective chemicals.

Wild onions are a traditional medicine of native North Americans for the treatment of colds, stings and bites. Chinese herbalists use them in a poultice for boils, and in European folk medicine they have been used for anaemia, bronchitis and asthma, genito-urinary infections and premature ageing. A night on the tiles in Paris traditionally ends with a steaming bowl of onion soup to prevent the next day's hangover, while in East Anglia thick onion soup was once a favourite for treating chesty children.

Onions contain the enzyme allinase, which is released when you slice the bulb. The reaction of this chemical with sulphur

Tips

All onions need fairly firm ground – veteran gardeners would roll the beds with light or heavy rollers, depending on the conditions. You can compact your seedbed by tapping with the flat of your spade.

Chewing parsley will help to get rid of the smell of onions on your breath.

compounds in the onion used to get the blame for making you cry – but it's not true. Japanese researchers have discovered the real culprit – a previously unknown enzyme called lachrymatory-factor synthase. This enzyme is released when you cut the onion and reacts with amino acids, creating the irritant substance that gets into the eyes and starts the tears flowing.

Cultivation

Maincrop onions prefer an open, sunny position and rich, well-manured soil, but will grow almost anywhere. Dig over the bed, incorporate plenty of organic material and leave to overwinter. Then break up any large lumps and rake to a fine tilth.

Personally, I always grow onions from sets (small onions ready to plant), because they are less trouble than seed and mostly very reliable. If you are planting a large bed, it is much cheaper to start from seed, but in a small plot it won't make much difference. Sets don't need such a rich soil and should be planted in mid-spring, at intervals of 15cm (6in) in rows that are 30cm (12in) apart. Make sure you draw a little soil up to the neck of each bulb. Water only as needed and hoe frequently but gently to remove weeds without

WHY EAT ONIONS?

VITAMIN C Good source. One large onion supplies 20 per cent of your daily requirement.
VITAMIN B6 Good source. The same large onion supplies 10 per cent of your daily requirement.
FIBRE Good source – again, the large onion supplies 10 per cent of your daily requirement.
MINERALS Onions contain useful quantities of manganese and potassium.
ANTIBACTERIAL, ANTI-INFLAMMATORY, ANTIFUNGAL Full of these medicinal properties.

REDUCED RISK OF CLOTTING

In one of my favourite experiments, we gave a group of volunteers a breakfast of fried eggs and bacon. Half of them also got a portion of fried onions. Blood tests then measured the clotting tendency of both groups. Without the onions there was increased risk of clotting; with them, a reduced one. So if you fancy a fry up, don't forget the onions.

HOW TO COOK

Onions are almost certainly the most widely used vegetable throughout the world. From the tiniest, grown indoors for salads, to the giants produced for competitions, they're used raw, boiled, pickled, sautéed or deep-fried. Add them to dishes for their taste and texture or serve them as a separate vegetable, boiled in a white sauce or roasted in a little oil.

disturbing the soil around the root or body of the onions. A special onion hoe is the best tool to use. As they grow, thin the early shoots to a distance of 10cm (4in). Thin them again later if required, and use those you pull up in salads.

If you prefer to start from scratch, plant the seeds in furrows, or drills, from late winter to early spring, to a depth of 2cm (¾in) and cover them lightly with some fine soil. The drills should be 30cm (12in) apart. Alternatively, you could plant your seeds in trays in midwinter, keep in a cold frame, under protective fleece or in a cool greenhouse, and once they have had a week or two of fresh air to harden off, plant out in drills as described. Start by putting the seedlings out for a few hours if the conditions are suitable, then increase little by little up to a full 24 hours.

For early crops, plant seed in drills at the end of summer and leave in situ until early spring. Then transplant into a prepared bed so they can mature sooner than the main crop. Some of the yellow Japanese onions are well suited to overwintering, but find the best for your region.

Shallots

Smaller than maincrop onions, shallots enjoy the same soil and growing conditions and are, likewise, easier to grow from sets than from seed. They are cultivated in the same way as onions, but each small bulb produces a cluster of new shallots, in the same way as garlic, rather than just one onion. Their mild, sweeter flavour makes it really worth growing these delicious bulbs, which are a staple in all French kitchens and perfect for pickling. Try to find the large, slightly pink, elongated shallots for their subtle flavour. Plant in late winter and harvest in midsummer. Dry and store just like onions.

Lifting and storing

By mid- to late summer you should have well-formed bulbs, and the green tops should be starting to bend. This is the time to help them ripen by bending the tops right over and when they start to shrivel around the neck and turn yellow, they are ready to lift. Take care not to bruise the bulbs. If the weather is dry and sunny, lay them out on the soil to dry naturally. If it looks like rain, keep them off the

TAKE TIME TO CHOOSE

Select the varieties you are going to grow with care. Soil conditions, seasons and climate all have to be taken into account. Your local garden centre, gardening society or gardening neighbours will, no doubt, be happy to point you in the right direction. Remember that some old-fashioned heritage plants may have better resistance to the pests and diseases that can attack the onion family. You will also find good information in leading plant, seed and bulb catalogues.

ONION FACTS

DON'T CRY!

There are lots of old wives' tales about how to stop onions making you cry. Try any of these:

1 Refrigerate the onions first, and start cutting at the pointed end, finishing at the root.
2 Peel onions under water.
3 Cut the onion in half, put it face down on a double layer of kitchen paper and leave for 15 minutes before chopping.
4 Sprinkle vinegar on your chopping board before you start.

5 Hold a piece of bread in between your teeth so that some of it sticks out under your nose. The bread will absorb the fumes before they get to your eyes.
6 Wear swimming goggles!
7 Light a candle beside the chopping board – the heat will attract the irritant vapours.
8 Always use a very sharp knife – a blunt one bruises the onion's flesh and releases more of the chemicals.
Personally, I don't bother with any of these – a few tears clean out the ducts anyway.

ground in an airy shed or lean-to, preferably with some direct sun.

Store your onions and shallots tied up by their necks in bunches in an airy, frost-free shed or garage and they will last through to your next early crop. Make sure they are not touching any walls.

Other varieties

Spring onions (scallions) are so easy to grow that every garden should have a small patch or a pot or two. Red and white varieties are available and have different flavours. Some Japanese ones can grow nearly as big as thin leeks, and hardy, overwintering varieties liven up any salad.

Sow normal types thinly, directly into a well-prepared bed in short rows of 30cm (12in). The rows should be 15cm (6in) apart. For a continuous supply, sow at 10-day intervals from early spring to late summer.

French white onions can be planted from late summer through to spring. Before they form the traditional white bulbs, use them as you would spring onions. Otherwise, leave them to mature and then either eat them raw or use in cooking.

Welsh onions are grown for their green, hollow leaves, which can be snipped and used like chives, although they taste like garlic – great in stews and salads, and with fish and poultry. By snipping into plastic bags, the leaves can be frozen to use in cooking when the fresh plants are not available. Like chives, the edible flowers are also delicious and decorative. Plant the seed in spring. Once established, the hardy perennial clumps can be carefully split and distributed to other pots or plots. They look good grown alongside roses and

lavender, or in the salad patch with lettuce and carrots. These unusual onions are perfect in a pot or tub on your balcony or terrace.

Egyptian, or tree, onions are very different – they produce very small bulbs at the end of their leaves after flowering. Plant the bulbs in their clumps in spring and wait. You may not get any onions in the first year. The plants can grow up to 1.5m (5ft) tall and are best staked for protection from wind. The small bulbs have a delicate flavour that goes well with fish, and they make very good onion-flavoured vinegar.

GOOD ADVICE

My 90-year-old French neighbour showed me how to make drills of an even depth by laying a cane, 2.5cm (1in) in diameter, on the ground and then treading it into the soil. Remove the cane and sow your seed in the resulting dip. It will all be at the same depth, so the onions will grow at the same rate.

Leeks

Leeks have a strong antibacterial effect and help to protect against stomach cancer, destroying some of the bacteria in the gut that change harmless nitrates into cancer-causing nitrites. In addition, they contain virtually no fat or salt and very little sugar, so it really helps to include leeks as a regular part of your diet if you're trying to lose weight.

This member of the onion family has been cultivated for at least 4,000 years as both food and medicine. Ancient Egypt was once described as a country in which 'onions are adored and leeks are gods'. The Greeks and Romans held them in the highest esteem, especially for the treatment of throat and voice problems. The infamous Emperor Nero ate leeks every day to improve the quality of his singing voice, and in French folk medicine leek soup was a traditional prescription for all breathing problems. Famed the world over for their male voice choirs, the Welsh adopted the leek as their national emblem, and many Welshmen wear one on St David's Day.

For anyone suffering from gout or arthritis, leeks are an ideal food because they help the body get rid of uric acid. Don't throw away all the dark green leafy bits – they're a great source of betacarotene (which is transformed internally into vitamin A) and other protective plant chemicals.

Cultivation

Leeks are hardy, do not take up much room and are easily grown in well-manured soil. Seed can be planted in a prepared bed in early spring when the risk of frost has past. By midsummer the seedlings will be about

Tips

All of the onion family, the Alliums, are subject to a number of diseases and pests, but good soil, clean conditions and care of your crops with the appropriate organic fertilizers will help build better resistance and strong plants.

Regular and careful hoeing is important – as the 'old boys' say, the time to hoe is when you can't see any weeds.

15cm (6in) tall and ready to transplant. Alternatively, you can buy the plants ready to go into your main bed.

Use a dibber to make a hole for each plant, 15cm (6in) deep and at intervals of 15cm (6in). The rows should be 36cm (18in) apart.

Do not replace the soil around the plants when you put them into the holes. Just fill each planted hole with water as soon as you have placed your leek in position. Nature will do the rest. Leeks will stand through the winter weather and get fatter month by month. For the most delicate taste and texture, try some early on when they are no thicker than your finger. If you choose a mixture of varieties, you will be eating fresh leeks from late summer right through to the end of the following spring.

Lifting and storing

Leeks are best pulled when the soil is damp. Hold each one as close to the earth as you can and tug. If you need to lift them from compacted soil, use a flat-bladed fork – the French call them spade forks.

Harvest only what you need for a few days, because the best way to store your leeks is in the ground. They will do well at

WHY EAT LEEKS?

VITAMINS K, A AND C Three medium-sized leeks will give you a whole day's supply of vitamin K, 75 per cent of vitamin A and 25 per cent of vitamin C. **VITAMIN B6 AND FOLIC ACID** Good source. **MINERALS** A good source of manganese and iron.

HOW TO COOK

I think, without doubt, that leeks are one of the most valuable of all winter vegetables, a true Superfood from the garden. They're not only supremely healthy, with a fabulous flavour, they're also extremely versatile in the kitchen. As a vegetable dish, you can braise, steam, griddle, roast, boil or stir-fry them. They're equally at home as the basic starting point for many soups and stews – often combined with their close relations, onion and garlic.

temperatures as low as 5°C, even covered in snow. If you expect much colder weather, apply a deep mulch, but do not let it come above the first leaf joint. If you do, the mulch will fall into the leek. If you cut off the roots and most of the leaves, you can store leeks in boxes of peat or sharp sand, but for a few weeks only and I don't think it's worth the effort.

It is possible to freeze leeks, but again, by the time they are trimmed, washed and blanched, is it worthwhile? A better option is to cook them first – make soup, leek tarts or ratatouille, or braise them before freezing, so each dish is ready to reheat.

VICHYSSOISE

Leek and potato soup served cold and sprinkled with chives is the invention of Louis Diat, who started as chef at the Ritz Carlton Hotel in New York in 1910. The inspiration came from the leek and potato soup his mother and grandmother used to make. He remembered how he and his brother used to cool the soup in summer by adding cold milk, and he decided to make something similar for his patrons. The now classic soup was named after the town of Vichy in France, close to the place where the boys grew up.

Chives and garlic chives

Chives and garlic chives, both members of the Allium family, are ancient medicinal herbs. They have been used in Chinese medicine for around 5,000 years but remained unknown in the western world until the extraordinary thirteenth-century explorer Marco Polo brought them back to Italy with all his other discoveries. Now they grow wild in Europe and Asia.

From the early seventeenth century, herbalists in England used chives to treat bladder problems. Now they are nearly always used as a decorative garnish and for their unmistakable but mild flavour. Garlic chives, also known as Chinese chives, have a flatter leaf than ordinary chives and, not too surprisingly, a pronounced garlic taste.

The stems and flowers of both plants can be eaten and both plants have the same cancer and heart-protective benefits as garlic and onions, but to a much lesser degree. They are an extremely rich source of some nutrients – the flowers are full of betacarotene – but are not usually eaten in large quantities. You wouldn't often consume more than a tablespoon of finely chopped chives at any one time.

Cultivation

Chives can be grown from seed but they have a long germination time and need careful watering – not too much or too little. Sow them in a heated propagator or in warm soil from late spring to early summer.

I prefer to buy ready-grown plants, and small pots of chives are available at almost any time of year. Provided that the leaves are green with no withered or yellowing tips, they should thrive when you replant

My friend Sarah gave me a super birthday present while I was writing this book – a multi-bladed pair of scissors. They are designed to snip chives very finely in the blink of an eye, and they work just as well on the flowers. Adding the petals to a sour-cream filling makes the best jacket potato you have ever tasted.

them. Chives do best in rich, moist soil and in sunny places, but will tolerate most soils and positions.

To keep your chives in perfect condition, cut them down to just above the ground two or three times a year, and remove the flowers at regular intervals to encourage growth. Spread by dividing clumps in autumn, and pot up some small clumps to keep on a sunny windowsill during the winter. Don't forget to keep trimming your indoor pots and give them some liquid feed once a month.

Ready-grown garlic chives are not always so easily found in nurseries or garden centres, but planting them as bulbs works well. They do best if you cut them little and often. Leave them to dry out between watering and feed monthly with a good organic liquid feed.

WHY EAT CHIVES AND GARLIC CHIVES?

VITAMINS K, C AND A Excellent source.
FOLIC ACID Good source.
FIBRE Good source, but you would need to eat enormous amounts to make much difference.
BETACAROTENE The flowers of both plants are a good source of betacarotene.

HARVESTING AND STORING

You can't dry chives like other herbs, but if you cut a reasonable-sized bunch and wrap the bottom in a piece of wet cotton wool, they will stay fresh in a plastic bag in the salad compartment of a fridge for up to a week.

You could also fill an ice tray with water, snip some chives into each compartment and freeze. Once solid, remove the cubes and store in a plastic bag in the freezer. Simply add a few cubes to soups, stews and casseroles at the end of cooking.

HOW TO COOK

Use the green stems, either finely snipped with scissors or whole, in salads and egg dishes, and with cottage or cream cheese. Mixed with butter and a little lemon juice, they make a great addition to jacket potatoes, grilled meat, omelettes or scrambled eggs. Wait until the final stages of cooking before adding chives or garlic chives if you want to preserve the best of their taste.

Add the flowers to your salads, float on top of soups or use with fish dishes to enhance the flavours.

Greek garlic leg of lamb casserole with lentils

This is a delicious, traditional slow-roast Greek lamb dish with a hint of France because of the lentils. Lentils are one of the most ancient of all known legume crops and have been found in prehistoric excavations. Early man knew the survival value of this cheap pulse. When combined with any cereal food, such as wheat, barley or oats, lentils provide Superfood nutrition, forming a complete protein as good as any meat. Lamb can be very fatty, so ask your butcher to cut away most of the fat on the surface of the meat, as all French housewives (and their husbands) expect.

Serves 4–6

60ml (4 tbsp) olive oil

1 medium leg of lamb, preferably organic

6 cloves garlic, chopped

2 onions, sliced

125g (4^{1}/$_{2}$oz) green lentils – Puy lentils if you can get them

300ml (10fl oz) red wine

2 bay leaves

1 bouquet garni

pinch sea salt and freshly ground black pepper

Preheat the oven to 180°C/350°F/gas 4.

Heat half the olive oil in an ovenproof casserole dish. Add the lamb, brown until it's sealed all over, remove and set to one side.

Add the garlic, onion and seasoning to the dish, adding more oil if required. Sweat gently until transparent. Then add the lentils and stir for 5 minutes. Don't let the onions brown.

Return the lamb to the dish, and add the wine, bay leaves and bouquet garni. Cover and put in the oven for 1^{1}/$_{2}$ hours, adding water when needed.

Remove the lamb, wrap in foil and leave for 10 minutes. Transfer the lentils to the middle of a serving dish, carve the lamb into chunks and arrange on top of the lentils. Serve with haricot or runner beans or a green salad.

BENEFITS

- Lamb is an excellent source of protein, iron, zinc and B vitamins.
- Lentils are rich in protein, zinc and other minerals.

Rabbit and onions

This quick and easy recipe takes 10 minutes to prepare and only 20 to cook. Rabbit is cheap, extremely low in fat and has been country fare for centuries, but try to find organic, home-produced rabbit rather than frozen imports from the Far East. This recipe has just 105 calories per 100g (3^{1}/$_{2}$oz) or 320 calories per portion, and if you've never eaten rabbit, it is a healthy introduction.

Serves 4

2 tbsp olive oil

750g (1^{1}/$_{2}$lb) rabbit, cut into pieces

1 large onion, finely chopped

4 medium tomatoes, chopped

350ml (6fl oz) dry cider

handful fresh parsley, chopped

pinch sea salt and freshly ground black pepper

Heat the oil in a large saucepan or frying pan and fry the rabbit pieces until they're brown all over. Add the onion and stir for 2 minutes. Add the rest of the ingredients, cover and simmer for 20 minutes.

BENEFITS

- This dish is very rich in protein, zinc, selenium and B12.
- It's also a valuable source of vitamins C, E and B6.

Cod on a cushion of leeks

Not exactly fish and chips, but much healthier and so easy, this tastes really good and looks quite impressive, too. It has hardly any fat, but lots of easy-to-digest protein from the fish, and a surprising bonus from the redcurrants. They contain a massive amount of protective antioxidants, so you don't need to waste your money on exotic berries from South America or the foothills of the Himalayas, or the latest money-making scam from bogus food gurus.

Serves 4

60ml (4 tbsp) peanut oil

4 small leeks, washed thoroughly and cut diagonally

110g (4oz) redcurrants (usually 1 small punnet)

4 cod steaks

6 tbsp flour

Heat half the oil in a large frying pan and sauté the leeks gently, turning frequently until golden, but don't let them brown – about 20 minutes.

Add the redcurrants and stir until tender. Lower the heat, cover and simmer for about 20 minutes.

In another pan, heat the rest of the oil. Coat the cod steaks with the flour and cook in the oil for about 5 minutes each side.

Pile a cushion of leeks and redcurrants on each plate, put the cod on top and serve.

BENEFITS

- Pure protein from the fish.
- No saturated fat, heart protection from the leeks, anti-oxidants from the currants.

Spring onion and anchovy tart

This tart is extremely easy to make – ready-made pastry is fine. It tastes great warm, but I prefer it cold with a fresh green salad. Anchovies can be rather salty, and if this is the case, soak them in milk for 10 minutes first.

Serves 4

1 sheet ready-made shortcrust pastry

1 large bunch spring onions, halved or quartered lengthwise (depending on size), retaining about 2.5cm (1in) of the green tops

2 x 50g (2oz) cans or jars of anchovies in olive oil, rinsed well in cold water and dried

300ml (10fl oz) crème fraîche

2 free-range eggs

Preheat the oven to 220°C/425°F/gas 7.

Lightly butter an 18cm (7in) flan tin and line with the pastry. Arrange the spring onions in a spiral towards the edge, with an anchovy or two between each piece.

Beat the crème fraîche with the eggs until smooth. Pour the mixture over the spring onions and anchovies. Bake for about 30 minutes until firm.

TIP: This tart looks good and tastes better if the surface browns slightly, but be careful not to burn the pastry.

Baked fish Provençal

This is such a healthy dish. It can be made from any thick white fish, such as hake, cod or haddock. With loads of onions and garlic and no saturated fat, it's not only a heart protector and a brain booster, but perfect for anyone suffering with high cholesterol, high blood pressure or any form of heart disease. You get a bonus from using canned tomatoes because they have more lycopene than fresh.

Serves 4

750g (1½lb) skinned thick fillets of fish

2 tbsp dry white wine

juice of 1 lemon

1 tbsp olive oil

1 onion, finely chopped

4 cloves garlic, finely chopped

400g (14oz) can chopped tomatoes

½ tsp herbes de Provence

12 pitted black olives, rinsed

2 tsp capers, rinsed

2 bay leaves

fresh parsley, chopped, to garnish

Marinate the fish in the white wine and lemon juice for at least an hour. Preheat the oven to 200°C/400°F/gas 6.

Heat the oil gently and sweat the onion and garlic. Remove the fish from the marinade and add the liquid to the onion and garlic. Stir for 5 minutes to reduce slightly. Then add the tomatoes, herbs, olives, capers and bay leaves.

Lightly oil an ovenproof dish, put in the fish, pour over the sauce and bake for 15–20 minutes. Sprinkle with parsley and serve.

Garlic, onion and tomato chutney in a millefeuille of sliced tomato

This is a cornucopia of all the best and most powerful antioxidants. It contains lycopene from the tomatoes, especially the cooked ones in the chutney; cholesterol-lowering chemicals from the garlic and onion; betacarotene; and plenty of vitamin C. All this comes from an original, cheap and easy recipe that looks four-star Michelin impressive.

BENEFITS

- Tomatoes contain lycopene.
- Chemicals in garlic and onion lower cholesterol.
- Dish also contains betacarotene and vitamin C.

Serves 4

450g (1lb) cherry tomatoes

1 red onion, peeled

2 cloves garlic, peeled

10 pitted black olives

2 good sprigs coriander

110g (4oz) demerara sugar

100ml (3¹/₂fl oz) cider vinegar

¹/₃ tsp quatre épices (four spice) powder

salt and freshly ground black pepper

4 large, round tomatoes

4 sprigs basil

Halve the cherry tomatoes. Whizz for 10 seconds in a processor, but leave a bit chunky. Whizz together the onion, garlic, olives and coriander. Put all the ingredients, except the large tomatoes and the basil, in a thick-bottomed saucepan and cook gently for around 20 minutes. Keep stirring until the mixture thickens into the consistency of chutney.

Cut each large tomato in horizontal slices and discard the bottom slice. Rebuild each tomato on a separate plate, putting a layer of chutney between each slice and top with a sprig of basil.

Serve with a small pot of the surplus chutney on each plate, baby new potatoes and some good, crusty bread.

Red onions with fromage blanc

This is a delicious way to eat one of nature's top Superfoods – baking sweet red onions with cider vinegar and adding a simple, healthy sauce. Fromage blanc contains generous amounts of bone-building calcium and is very similar to fromage frais, which may be easier to find in some places. The sauce is good with most vegetables and also poured over plainly cooked fish, meats or poultry.

BENEFITS

- Onions contain fibre, vitamin C, vitamin B6, potassium and heart-protective chemicals.
- Fromage blanc is rich in calcium.
- Caraway seeds are a great digestive aid and help reduce flatulence.
- Chives, parsley and lemon juice provide vitamin C.

Serves 4

4 large red onions, peeled until you reach the shiny flesh

1 tbsp cider vinegar

1 tsp brown sugar

juice of $\frac{1}{2}$ lemon

150g (5oz) low-fat fromage blanc

1 tsp Dijon mustard

$\frac{1}{2}$ tsp caraway seeds

2 tbsp mixed chives and curly parsley, finely chopped

salt and freshly ground black pepper

Preheat the oven to 180°C/350°F/gas 4.

Cut a slice off the base of the onions so that they stand level, and then cut a deep cross in each one, but make sure they stay intact. Wrap each onion in foil, place in an ovenproof dish and bake for 50 minutes.

Open the foil, season with salt and pepper, add the vinegar and sugar and return to the oven for 15 minutes.

Mix the lemon juice with the fromage blanc, mustard, caraway seeds and herbs. Take the onions out of the oven, remove from the foil on to plates and pour the sauce over the top.

Serve with fried fish, grilled meat or poultry.

Shallots in red wine

OK, so this recipe contains butter, but food needs to taste good and there are no substitutes – least of all the awful margarines that were supposed to be healthy but contain transfats. They are more likely to cause heart problems than natural butter. Anyway, the red wine and the shallots are a major protection against heart disease and lots more besides.
If you can find them, use the long French shallots. They are less sharp than the small round varieties.

Serves 4

110g (4oz) unsalted butter

450g (1lb) medium-sized shallots, peeled

200ml (7fl oz) vegetable or herb stock, preferably home-made

200ml (7fl oz) red wine

1 tbsp runny honey – thyme honey if you can get it

2 large sprigs fresh thyme

Heat half the butter in a large pan. Tip in the shallots and cook, shaking gently, until golden brown all over. Pour in the stock and simmer until reduced to just a few tablespoonsful. Pour in the wine, honey and thyme and boil down gently again.

Off the heat, add the rest of the butter, cut into cubes, and stir carefully until the shallots are glazed.

BENEFITS

- The red wine and shallots provide protection for the heart.
- Thyme contains thymol, an antibacterial essential oil.

Leeks vinaigrette with capers and anchovies

This is an amazing way to use later leek thinnings, and the best reason of all to pick finger-thick baby leeks from the garden. Tender, succulent and bursting with nutrients, they are the perfect match for anchovies and capers. Capers are the real surprise. They aren't just a bit of decoration on the side! Caper extract, too, is rich in antioxidants and, even in small amounts as flavouring, has the same protective effect as vitamin E. When added to a burger, caper extract helps prevent the formation of certain meat by-products that are linked to increased risk of some cancers and heart disease.

Serves 4

3 tbsp extra virgin olive oil

3 tbsp hazelnut oil

3 tbsp white wine vinegar

1/2 tsp Dijon mustard

8 young leeks

500ml (18fl oz) vegetable stock

1 tbsp capers

50g (2oz) can anchovies

5 tbsp fresh parsley, finely chopped

First, make the dressing by mixing the oils, vinegar and mustard and whisking thoroughly.

Wash and clean the leeks and simmer in the stock until tender – about 15 minutes.

Meanwhile, rinse the capers in running water and soak the anchovies in milk, if necessary, to get rid of the salt. Drain on kitchen paper.

Arrange the leeks on a serving plate with the capers and anchovies on top, pour on the dressing and scatter with the parsley. Enjoy this dish just warm or at room temperature, but not straight from the fridge, because you will lose most of the flavour.

BENEFITS

- Leeks contain antioxidants and betacarotene.
- Capers are rich in antioxidants.
- Anchovies contain omega-3 fatty acids.
- The oils contain cholesterol-reducing, mono-unsaturated fats.

Leek and sorrel tarts

This dish combines all the heart and circulation benefits of leeks with betacarotene and iron from the sorrel. If sorrel is hard to find in your neighbourhood, it is really worth growing your own, maybe in a largish pot. However, keep off the sorrel if you have gout or kidney stones because it contains a lot of oxalic acid, which can aggravate these conditions. Spinach is a good substitute.

BENEFITS

- Leeks contain antioxidants and betacarotene.
- Sorrel contains betacarotene and iron.

Serves 2

1 packet shortcrust pastry

350g (12oz) young leeks, washed and finely chopped

organic rapeseed oil

6 sorrel leaves

1 pinch quatre épices (four spice) powder

300ml (10fl oz) béchamel sauce

freshly ground black pepper

Preheat the oven to 200°C/400°F/gas 7.

Roll out the pastry and bake blind in 4 small, non-stick tart dishes for 10 minutes. To bake blind, put the pastry into the well-greased dishes, prick the base several times with a fork, then cover with baking beans (small ceramic beans available from cook shops), or use dried chick peas. This allows the pastry to cook without the sides falling in or the bottom rising too much. Leave to cool slightly.

While the pastry's baking, gently sauté the leeks in the oil and season with pepper. Stir in the sorrel leaves and spice powder.

Put the leeks and sorrel into the pastry tarts, pour over the béchamel sauce and return to the oven for 15 minutes.

Grilled salmon with leeks and Parmesan

Here is more proof that healthy food can also be delicious. The idea comes from one of our elderly French neighbours, an 84-year-old farmer's wife. Her grandson fishes for trout in the local river and she grows leeks in her weed-free kitchen garden – I see her hoeing at six in the morning. Sally made the same dish, but used wild salmon from our village fishmonger. This excellent meal will take just 45 minutes from start to finish.

BENEFITS

- Salmon is super-rich in omega-3 fats, which have powerful anti-inflammatory properties.
- Leeks contain antioxidants and betacarotene.

Serves 4

2 medium leeks

1 tbsp olive oil

125ml (4fl oz) dry white wine

200ml (7fl oz) crème fraîche

4 tbsp salted butter

4 fillets of fresh salmon

grated Parmesan

sea salt and freshly ground black pepper

Preheat the grill to maximum.

Wash the leeks well, dry and cut into small chunks. Sweat them gently in the oil but do not brown. When soft, add the wine to the pan to deglaze (dilute and thin) the cooking juices, then add the crème fraîche to make the sauce, and keep warm.

Rub 1 tablespoon of butter into both sides of each piece of salmon, season and griddle until just brown and crisp on both sides. Cover with the sauce, sprinkle with Parmesan and grill until the cheese is brown and bubbling.

Serve hot from the grill accompanied by a green, minty salad.

chapter 3
legumes

peas • runner beans • French beans
• broad beans

Peas

Although many of us eat more peas than any other vegetable apart from potatoes, the tragedy is that often they are canned and even more are frozen, losing nutrients and flavour. Growing your own is a totally different story. Peas do take a bit of space in the garden, but it is worth it because they are such a versatile crop, delicious when freshly picked, and so good for you.

Strangely, we know little of the origins of this valuable food crop. The Greeks and Romans had many varieties, and evidence of peas has been found in Bronze Age excavations. Wild peas were popular in medieval Britain, and by the late sixteenth century several varieties were known to herbalists. Later, the pinnacle of gardening achievement was to pick your first early crop of peas on 4 June, George III's birthday. Today we have so much choice that you can plan to eat fresh peas from mid-spring through to late autumn.

Sugars in peas start changing into starches as soon as the pods are picked, and many people prefer the sweeter taste of peas that are frozen in the field. When you buy them from the supermarket or greengrocer, they are days old. Nothing matches the wonderful flavour of home-grown peas, which is why you need to sow them in succession for a long season.

Cultivation

For an early crop, sow hardy varieties, which will need protection with cloches or a polytunnel. You can plant into modules, keep indoors until they germinate, then harden off and plant *in situ*. I like to germinate early peas in a pot, sowing them around the rim. When they shoot, put them outside for a few

Choosing varieties
What types you choose to grow and when you sow them will depend on where you live and the local climate. If you are new to an area, or a novice gardener, ask the neighbours or go to the local allotment. Gardeners are a friendly and chatty lot, except where competitions are involved. You will be amazed at how much help, advice, and even seeds and cuttings, you will be given.

hours at a time, then permanently so they harden off. When ready to plant, tip out the pot gently, then unroll the ball of compost and seedlings along a prepared ridge of soil, push into the top, earth up and water.

For the second early crop, first make a shallow trench by pressing a length of guttering into your prepared soil. Remove the guttering and block its ends with masking tape. Fill the guttering with potting compost and plant your peas in it, 8cm (3in) apart. Keep in a cool greenhouse, tunnel or a very sheltered place in the garden. When your peas are about 5cm (2in) high, remove the tape from one end and carefully ease the whole lot into the trench you made in the soil.

Your main crop should be sown in four lots at three-week intervals, but depending on the weather, the results can be very different. This year, for instance, my second and third sowings were ready before the first one. Early spring was very hot and peas prefer to be a bit cooler, which is just what they got later on. Don't overwater your peas because they will grow too fast and become leggy.

When the crop is over, cut off the tops and add to compost (if there is any sign of mildew, burn them). The roots have little nitrogen-fixing nodules, so leave them in the soil and dig them in later.

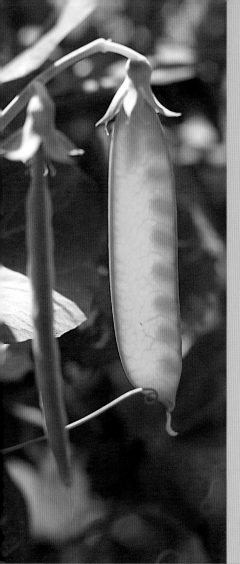

WHY EAT PEAS?

VITAMIN A Useful source. Sugarsnap and mangetout peas are great varieties because you eat the entire pod, so you get lots more vitamins A and C as well as some extra fibre.
VITAMIN B1 (THIAMIN) Excellent source – 150g (5oz) of fresh peas supplies more than a day's requirement.
VITAMIN C Useful source.
FIBRE Excellent source of the special soluble fibre that helps to lower cholesterol and is good for the digestive system.
FOLIC ACID Good source. Folic acid is vital for heart health and during pregnancy.
PROTEIN Peas and all beans provide good amounts of protein.

HARVESTING AND STORING

Pick peas as soon as the pods are full and bright green, and mangetout as soon as they're a decent size and crisp enough to snap in half. If you want to dry your peas, leave them on the vines until the end of the season, when they will be brown and papery. Harvest the entire plant, tie in bunches by the roots and hang in the garage, shed or greenhouse. Once the pods are easy to open, put the peas in airtight jars.

HOW TO COOK

As with most other vegetables, eat peas as soon after picking as possible, when they are at their freshest and bursting with goodness. Vitamins B and C are destroyed by heat, so boil for just long enough to soften the texture, and use the cooking water in gravies, stocks or soups. If you are having to buy peas, rather than growing your own, it's good to know that modern freezing conserves both sweetness and most of the vitamin C, and there is minimal nutrient loss for about a year. However, cook frozen peas in the minimum amount of water for as short a time as possible, otherwise the losses become significant.

Pea supports

Peas need supporting, and while traditional twigs look rustic, they are a pain! Make life simple and use pea netting or if, like me, you are a recycling fanatic, use old wire fence or chicken wire.

Put some sturdy stakes in at the ends and middle of your row, fix the netting to them, then add canes, threaded through the net for extra strength.

Make a shallow trench on each side of the netting. Plant a row of seeds on each side, water in and wait.

The plants will bush out and grow up the supports. You can use double rows of supports with the peas in the middle, but I find the crop more difficult to pick.

Runner beans and French beans

Nutritionally, runner beans and French beans are almost the same. Both are eaten when the pods are young and before large beans have formed inside them. The scarlet flowers of runner beans are distinctive, making them a very attractive feature in any garden. French beans don't grow so tall, but have a surprising number of varieties.

Traditionally, runner beans were called scarlet runners, and this variety is the best known, although white- and pink-flowered versions are available. The runner bean originates from Central and South America, and in Mexico the starchy root is still used in cooking. French beans come from that region, too.

To me, French beans meant just the pencil-sized green beans growing on small, bushy plants until I came to live in France. Then I discovered a whole world of different varieties, each used in its own way. My neighbour has early beans for eating whole; later ones for preserving; another variety for drying, keeping the inner beans to eat with traditional recipes throughout the winter; purple and yellow ones that crop later; and, finally, a flat type that looks like a runner bean with smooth skin, but has no strings, and climbs up poles.

Caution
The actual beans of both runner and French beans, fresh and dried, contain some of the chemical group known as lectins. These can cause stomach upsets if eaten raw, so it's always best to cook the pods.

Growing French beans

French beans like a light but well-manured soil, and need some protection from cold winds. Unlike runner beans, I find all French beans do best if grown inside in deep trays or old wooden boxes – I scrounge around the shops for empty wine boxes. You can buy ready-to-use plugs in their own plastic bases, and although these cost a bit more, they pretty well guarantee 100 per cent germination as long as you start with good-quality seed.

When seedlings are large enough to handle, and there is no risk of frost, plant them out from mid-spring, leaving 15cm (6in) between each plant. At the same time, sow more seed directly into the soil, 15cm (6in) apart and at a depth of 5cm (2in). Carry on sowing at three-week intervals through to late summer for harvesting up to early winter, weather permitting.

French beans need regular watering, especially once the flowers appear. In a dry spell you must give them copious amounts of water if you want to avoid tough, stringy beans on your plate. Once they start to grow well, earth up the stems to prevent the roots coming loose in the wind, then give them a good mulch to help retain moisture.

> **TIP**
> Leave some of the larger runner bean pods on the vines to mature. Then pick them, extract the beans and store them in a sealed, airtight jar to plant next year.

WHY EAT RUNNER BEANS & FRENCH BEANS?

VITAMINS A, C AND K A good source of all these vitamins. Their vitamin A content makes them useful in the treatment of all skin disorders.
FIBRE Both contain enough fibre to help with constipation.
MINERALS Useful quantities of copper, potassium, calcium and iron.
B VITAMINS Useful amounts.
PLANT HORMONES Like all legumes, they contain some beneficial plant hormones, which means they may be helpful in the relief of menstrual problems, PMT and the hot flushes associated with the menopause.
PROTEIN Both are good sources of protein.

HARVESTING AND STORING

Runner beans: Harvest every two days to make sure they do not get tough and fibrous. If you water regularly and give them a liquid feed once a fortnight, you can eat, freeze or bottle the beans through to the autumn.
French beans: Eat or freeze as soon as possible after picking. To dry beans, leave the pods on the plant until they start to turn brown, then pull the whole plant and tie upside down in a cool, dry, airy shed or garage. When the pods have dried, take out the beans. Store in rubber-sealed, spring-top, airtight jars. Keep cool and out of sunlight. Don't keep in plastic containers, because these may taint the flavour, and the beans might sweat, causing mould.
Dried French beans (haricot): Although they lose a lot of their vitamin content when dried, they are richer than fresh beans in protein and minerals.

HOW TO COOK

Once picked, fresh beans will keep in the fridge for a few days, but quickly become limp and tasteless. Wash, top and tail, then steam or add to already boiling water and cook for the shortest possible time – they should be *al dente*. If you're keeping them to use cold in salads, refresh immediately in ice-cold water. If you leave them hot, they'll continue cooking and lose nutrients.

Growing runner beans

These can grow to 3m (10ft) tall. They need solid support so they are not blown over by strong winds as they start to put on leaf growth. I like to grow them up a cane wigwam, in a sunny, sheltered spot.

Dig lots of organic matter into the soil. Push 6–8 tall canes into the ground, using a measuring stick to ensure they are evenly spaced.

Gently pull the tops of the canes together and tie firmly with a length of garden string.

Plant 2 seeds at the base of each cane once the soil is warm, about 12°C (53°F). Plant in late spring and you will pick your first beans by midsummer.

Water well and keep the soil moist. The plants will produce tendrils that will wind around the canes, and the beans will hang down inside the canes.

Broad beans

Nothing gives me quite so much pleasure as picking my first broad beans of the year in the middle of spring, having planted them in late autumn. Unless you live in an area of severe winter frosts, it's always worth planting an autumn crop. For some reason, these are much more resistant to blackfly, and unless there's an exceptionally hard winter, most will survive.

Broad beans, properly known as fava beans, are one of the most nutritious vegetables, so why does Pythagoras advise us not to eat them? It's amazing that the two great philosophers Pythagoras and Aristotle should have argued about them in the sixth century BCE.

The answer is a fascinating and rare disease called favism. This genetic disorder is found in parts of the ancient Greek empire around the Mediterranean, where up to 30 per cent of the population still carry the disease. It's most common in males, and eating broad beans, or even smelling the scent from the flowers of a growing crop, is enough to trigger a severe form of haemolytic anaemia that causes jaundice, kidney failure and often death. On some Mediterranean islands, it's forbidden to grow fava beans, let alone eat them.

The upside is that the condition is linked to a gene that enables those who have favism to survive malaria, which may not sound like much until you realize that as late as the 1940s there were 100,000 cases of malaria in one year on the island of Sardinia alone.

Heady perfume
The small white flowers of broad beans have an extraordinary smell that will pervade your garden on spring and early summer evenings. Unfortunately, this is bad news for people with favism since just a sniff can make them very ill.

Cultivation

Broad beans are best sown about 20cm (8in) apart, in double rows, leaving about 20cm (8in) between the two rows and 1 metre (39in) between each pair. I grow a very old variety called Aquadulce Claudia, which is perfect for sowing in late autumn or late winter and produces delicious white beans for late spring and early summer picking. If space is a problem, grow a bush variety, such as Sutton Large. These are exceptionally hardy, grow to about 30cm (12in), and can be sown outdoors in early spring or under cloches at the end of autumn.

As the beans grow, they're liable to wind damage, so support them with canes down each side of the plants and string from cane to cane all the way round.

Keep an eagle eye for blackfly, and spray with non-toxic derris or soap solutions at the first sign.

When you have finished harvesting your beans, cut the plants at soil level and add to the compost heap, leaving the roots where they are. In common with all legumes, the roots replenish soil nitrogen, so dig them back into the soil.

WHY EAT BROAD BEANS?

PROTEIN Great source.
BETACAROTENE The betacarotene in broad beans is converted into a valuable amount of vitamin A.
VITAMINS C AND B Broad beans contain useful amounts of vitamin C and also some of the B vitamins, including folate (B9) and riboflavin (B2).
MINERALS They supply potassium, calcium and iron as well as copper and manganese.
FIBRE Broad beans are rich in fibre, and contain no fat or cholesterol, or salt. They have just 80 calories per 100g (3½oz).

HARVESTING AND STORING

Pick every few days. Don't store the pods in the fridge because they soon go black and slimy. Instead, keep in a cool, airy space away from direct sun, but eat within a few days.

Broad beans freeze exceptionally well, but only freeze them when young. Pod them, bag them and put straight into the freezer.

HOW TO COOK

Broad beans are at their most tender when they're fairly small. If you leave them on the plant too long, they get large and tough. Smart chefs peel the outer skin off the podded beans, but I think this is a waste of time and you lose fibre and nutrients. Pick them young and you'll have no problems.

They're best boiled with a sprig of the herb summer savory, which helps eliminate the flatulence factor. I never add salt to the cooking water because this can make the outer skins tough. These beans are wonderful added to stews and casseroles and just as delicious eaten cold with a vinaigrette dressing – and don't forget that the leafy tops make wonderful sweet spring greens, cooked in very little water or steamed. Canned broad beans lose half their vitamin C content, and a lot of their flavour.

Spanish omelette with beans and peas

I got the idea for this recipe when we had a particularly good crop of beans and peas last year, but it works equally well with your own defrosted veg in the middle of winter. If you want to end up with the traditional cake-like shape, use a smaller, deeper pan, which takes a little more care and trouble, but is worth the effort. We cook this at least once a week, and I always make sure there's enough to eat cold for breakfast the next day.

Serves 4

1 small onion, finely chopped

1 clove garlic, finely chopped

1 medium potato, peeled and cubed

2 tbsp olive oil

450g (1lb) mixed broad beans, runner beans, French beans and peas

8 large free-range eggs

freshly ground black pepper

pinch sea salt

pinch chilli powder

Gently sauté the onion, garlic and potato in the olive oil until softened but not brown. Blanch the beans and peas in boiling, unsalted water for 5 minutes, drain and add to the pan with the onions and potato. Cook gently for 5 minutes.

Beat the eggs gently, adding pepper, salt and chilli powder. Pour over the bean mixture in the pan, first adding a little more oil if necessary, and cook over the lowest possible heat until the edge sets and starts to come away from the pan. When the rest of the omelette is almost set and the bottom is starting to brown, place the pan under a very hot grill for 2–3 minutes.

Put a large plate over the pan and quickly turn both the plate and pan upside down. Shake gently so the omelette drops onto the plate. Leave to stand for 15 minutes before serving.

Spaghettini with peas and baby clams

As usual, Granny was right when she said you should eat fish for your brains – and we now know that it's essential to eat oily fish during pregnancy and while breast-feeding for optimum brain development in babies. There's no doubt that this classic Italian dish fits the bill admirably.

Serves 4

700g (1½lb) clams, rinsed thoroughly

225g (8oz) spaghettini

1 small onion, finely chopped

2 cloves garlic, finely chopped

55g (2oz) unsalted butter

2 tbsp extra virgin olive oil

112ml (4fl oz) dry white wine

225g (8oz) peas, fresh or frozen

1 large cup curly parsley, finely chopped

Simmer the clams, covered, in half a cup of water until they open. Take them out of the pan using a slotted spoon. Strain the liquor through muslin to remove any fine grit and reserve it.

Cook the pasta according to the packet instructions. Sweat the onion and garlic in the butter and oil. Add the wine, peas and clam liquor and boil for 5 minutes. Then add the clams. Season, stir in the parsley and pour over the pasta to serve.

TIP: You can remove the clams from their shells, but I think this dish is much more appealing – and more fun to eat – if they're left in them. This recipe is best made with dry pasta rather than fresh. It doesn't have to be spaghettini – choose your favourite.

Goujons of sole with green pea purée

Sole is a good choice for this recipe because each fillet will divide easily to make the individual strips (goujons), but if you can't get sole, any other white fish works just as well. They all taste fabulous with this Moroccan-inspired minted dip, which can, of course, also be served on its own with pitta bread and crudités. Do take the trouble to make your own breadcrumbs. All it takes is some stale wholemeal bread and a small electric grinder or an old-fashioned grater. If you make a decent batch, you can store it in the freezer ready for instant use, avoiding all the fat, salt, colourings and other additives in most commercial products.

Serves 4

2 shallots, chopped

2 cloves garlic, finely chopped

2 tbsp extra virgin olive oil

700g (1½lb) garden peas

12 fresh mint leaves

250ml (9fl oz) vegetable stock

juice of 1 lemon

pinch chilli powder

700g (1½lb) sole, cut into strips

2 free-range eggs, beaten

200g (7oz) wholemeal breadcrumbs

250ml (9fl oz) rapeseed oil

Sweat the shallots and garlic in the olive oil until they are soft but not brown. Add the peas, mint and stock and cook until the peas are just done. Allow to cool a little and then put the contents of the pan into a blender or food processor with the lemon juice and chilli powder, and whizz until smooth. Season to taste and set aside.

Dip the fish goujons first in the beaten egg, then in the breadcrumbs, and fry them in the rapeseed oil until crisp. If you don't have a deep fryer, use a wok. Drain on kitchen paper and serve with the dip on the side. This is equally delicious whether fish and dip are warm or cold.

BENEFITS

- Sole, in common with all fish, is full of protein, iodine and other minerals, and B vitamins.
- Fibre and betacarotene from the peas.
- Mint contains essential oils that are one of nature's all-time best digestive aids.

Cod paella with French beans and peas

Here is another Superfoods recipe with all the health benefits of onion, garlic and tomatoes. On a cold day, this tasty meal will transport you back to holidays spent in sunnier climes!

BENEFITS

- The prawns and cod in one helping provide 40 per cent of your daily requirement of protein, half the selenium you need, 20 per cent of the B12 and a good supply of iron and brain-nourishing omega-3.
- The beans and peas give you substantial amounts of fibre, vitamins C and K and a selection of B vitamins.
- Green pepper provides vitamin C.

Serves 4

2 tbsp olive oil

1 medium onion, finely sliced

2 cloves garlic, finely chopped

2 medium tomatoes, skinned, deseeded and chopped

1 medium green pepper, deseeded and finely chopped

700ml (1¼ pints) fish stock

125g (4½oz) prawns, cooked and peeled

175g (6oz) cod fillet cut into bite-sized pieces

175g (6oz) long grain rice

75g (3oz) French beans, trimmed and halved

75g (3oz) fresh or frozen peas

flat-leaf parsley to garnish

Heat half the oil in a large, wide saucepan – or paella pan if you have one – and gently sauté the onion and garlic until golden. Add the tomatoes and continue cooking for 4 minutes, stirring all the time. Purée the mixture and set aside.

Wipe the pan clean, heat the rest of the oil and add the green pepper. Cook until soft. Pour in the stock and add the onion mixture, prawns, cod, rice, French beans and peas. Simmer gently for about 20 minutes until all the stock has been absorbed. Serve the paella scattered with the parsley.

Broad bean and feta salad

Add a chunk of coarse, wholemeal bread, a glass of wine and some fresh fruit and you have a wonderful light lunch dish, the perfect combination of a well-balanced meal and pleasure! Despite the cheese, the total fat in this dish is only 10 per cent of the advised maximum daily consumption.

BENEFITS

- This salad is full of protein, carbohydrate and fats.
- It has an abundance of fibre, calcium, trace minerals and B vitamins.

Serves 4

275g (10oz) fresh broad beans, shelled weight

3 tbsp extra virgin olive oil

1 tbsp white wine vinegar

2 tbsp fresh mint, chopped

75g (3oz) feta cheese, cubed

Cook the beans in a pan of boiling water for 3–4 minutes until they are tender. Drain well and put into a bowl. Mix together the oil, vinegar and mint and stir into the hot beans. When the beans have cooled to room temperature, mix in the cubed feta and serve.

TIP: You can make this salad in advance, but try to avoid keeping it in the fridge because the oil will thicken and most of the delicate flavours will be lost.

Lamb parmentier

You may think this dish looks like a pudding with cream on top, but in fact it's a delicious, healthy take on the traditional shepherd's pie. It was served to me in a tiny bistro opposite the great food market in the beautiful French city of Tours, and I was captivated by the imaginative use made of the freshest possible ingredients, gathered from the market first thing each morning.

Serves 4

500g (1lb 2oz) potatoes

50g (2oz) butter

2 tbsp cream

nutmeg, two twists

110g (4oz) slightly salted butter

2 medium carrots, peeled and cubed

2 cloves garlic, finely chopped

2 medium shallots, finely chopped

600g (1¼lb) minced lean lamb

1 tbsp tomato purée

75g (3oz) fresh or frozen peas

1 bouquet garni – make your own by tying thyme, rosemary and bay leaves together with a piece of string

125ml (4fl oz) red wine

125ml (4fl oz) vegetable stock

Preheat the oven to 200°C/400°F/gas 6.

Steam or boil the potatoes and mash to a smooth purée with the butter, cream and nutmeg. Keep hot.

Put half the butter into a frying pan with the carrots, garlic and shallots. Cook gently for about 5 minutes until the vegetables are soft but not brown. Add the lamb, tomato purée, peas and bouquet garni, and sauté, stirring constantly, for another 5 minutes. Pour in the red wine and vegetable stock, stir well, bring to a simmer and leave to reduce for 15 minutes.

Remove the bouquet garni. Divide the lamb between four glass preserving jars. Top with the potato and put into the oven to heat through for about 10 minutes.

If you want to be more traditional, put the meat in an ovenproof dish, cover with the potato and cook in the preheated oven for 20 minutes.

Warm chicken salad with cranberries

There's no need to throw salads off the menu as soon as the clocks go back. Warm salads are delicious and satisfying, especially if you add croutons. This one has cold ingredients but a warm dressing and gives you all the benefits of fresh produce in the lettuce and parboiled beans, which retain most of their nutritional content.

BENEFITS

- Cranberries and olive oil have antioxidant properties, so this recipe helps both to protect your heart and to safeguard against cancer.

Serves 4

2 thick slices wholemeal bread, crusts removed

2 tbsp rapeseed oil

1 clove garlic, squashed, then finely chopped

175g (6oz) trimmed runner beans

2 skinless chicken breasts, cooked and cut into slivers

1 tight-headed lettuce, shredded

110g (4oz) cranberries

1 tbsp runny honey

2 tbsp olive oil

1 tbsp red wine vinegar

Cut the bread into 1cm (½in) cubes. Heat the rapeseed oil and sweat the garlic. Then add the bread and cook over a medium heat, stirring, until the cubes are golden. Drain them on kitchen paper, discard the oil and garlic and set the croûtons aside.

Simmer the runner beans in boiling water for 3 minutes, refresh in cold water and drain well. Arrange the chicken, beans and lettuce in four bowls.

Put the cranberries into a small saucepan, cover with water, add the honey and simmer for 3 minutes. Pour in the olive oil and red wine vinegar. Leave them to rest for 2 minutes, then pour over the salad. Garnish with the croûtons to serve.

TIP: You don't need to use extra virgin olive oil for cooking – it's expensive, so buy the best you can afford and save it for salad dressings. Ordinary 100 per cent olive oil is perfectly all right for recipes in which the oil will be heated.

Calves' liver and broad bean risotto

Risotto is another of my favourite dishes, and calves' liver has to be one of the most delicious foods ever, even though it is expensive. It takes just minutes to cook and has a wonderfully soft texture. It's also extremely healthy. Here, I've put the two together with all the extra protective nutrients of the broad beans to make a picture of a meal.

BENEFITS

■ Broad beans contain fibre and protein as well as B vitamins and minerals.
■ A single portion of calves' liver provides huge amounts of iron, copper, zinc, potassium and several days' worth of vitamins A, B12 and folic acid.

Serves 2

1 tbsp extra virgin olive oil

50g (2oz) unsalted butter

6 fresh sage leaves, finely chopped

175g (6oz) calves' liver, cut into fine slivers

250g (9oz) baby broad beans

1 small onion, thinly sliced

110g (4oz) risotto rice, preferably carnaroli

600ml (1 pint) vegetable stock, preferably home-made

3 tbsp single cream

Heat the oil and butter, add the sage and then the liver. Pan-fry for about 2 minutes, until the liver is brown on the outside but still pink in the middle. Remove from the pan and set aside.

Meanwhile, cook the broad beans in boiling, unsalted water until just tender. Drain and keep warm with the cooked liver.

Sweat the onion in the remaining oil and butter until just soft. Add the rice and stir until it is coated with the butter. Start adding the stock, a ladle at a time, stirring until the liquid is absorbed. Continue until the rice is almost tender.

Gently stir in the liver and broad beans and heat through for 1 minute, adding a little more stock if necessary. Stir in the cream to serve.

CAUTION: This dish is ideal for anyone with anaemia, and perfect if you are trying to get pregnant. Once you are expecting, though, it's best not to eat any liver or pâté because the very high levels of vitamin A could harm the developing baby.

Minted broad bean soup

Soups should be a regular feature in every kitchen. They are often quick and simple to make, delicious, comforting and extremely nutritious. This one is no exception, and mint is one of the best of all digestive aids. It is still a constituent of modern indigestion remedies. This soup is just what the doctor ordered if you, or someone you are cooking for, has problems with digestion.

BENEFITS

■ The broad beans in one steaming bowlful of this soup provide 20 per cent of your daily protein needs, half your daily requirement of folic acid and more than a quarter of copper and manganese, as well as a selection of B vitamins.

Serves 4

1 tbsp vegetable oil

1 onion, chopped

2 cloves garlic, chopped

2 medium potatoes, peeled and diced

500ml (18fl oz) vegetable stock

700g (1½lb) broad beans, shelled weight

juice of 1 lemon

300ml (10fl oz) single low-fat fromage frais or soya milk

1 large sprig mint, chopped

mint leaves to garnish

Heat the oil in a large pan, add the onions and garlic and cook until the onions begin to soften. Add the potatoes and stock to the pan and simmer for about 20 minutes, until the potatoes are cooked.

Meanwhile, cook the broad beans in boiling water for about 5 minutes, then drain and add to the stock mixture.

Leave the soup to cool slightly, then add the lemon juice, fromage frais and chopped mint. Purée until smooth. Season to taste, and reheat if necessary. Garnish with mint leaves.

chapter 4
root veg

carrots • potatoes • Jerusalem artichokes
• beetroot • parsnips • radishes

Carrots

Carrots, a favourite vegetable of the ancient Romans, seem like something of a miracle food. Eating them regularly reduces the incidence of many forms of cancer, heart disease, bowel disorders and lung disease, and they are good for your eyes and skin. But the main reason to eat carrots is for their wonderful taste.

Inevitably, carrots are at their best when they're in season and fresh. Very young carrots may look appealing in bunches with all their greenery, but mature carrots have far more betacarotene for your body to turn into vitamin A. Carrots are powerful antioxidant and anti-ageing vegetables. They help protect the skin against sun damage and wrinkles, and improve blood flow in the coronary arteries.

There are many varieties of carrots – which ones you choose to grow depends on your soil, and the ones you like best. They can be round and almost surface-growing, like shallots, for heavy soil; they can be short, long, thick or thin and come in a variety of cultivars for early and maincrop planting.

Cultivation

Carrots need a sunny, open position. Deep, fertile, sandy soil is good for the long

To prevent sowing carrot seeds too thickly, try mixing the seed with sharp sand before sprinkling along the drill.

varieties. Short-rooted varieties will grow well in slightly heavier soil. Do not add heavy manure to the soil; carrots grown in heavy soil or where organic matter is not well rotted will become misshapen. If your soil is unsuitable, try using growbags or containers. These are fine for carrots, but better suited to short-rooted varieties.

Sow outdoors in late spring, when frosts have passed and the soil has had time to warm up. If sowing under cover (greenhouse or cloche), sow in late winter or early spring.

Make a drill 1cm (½in) deep and sow seeds very thinly. Cover with a fine layer of soil, firm down gently and water in. Space the drills 15cm (6in) apart. Thin out seedlings when they are large enough to handle.

If you buy plants, space them 5 to 7.5cm (2 to 3in) apart. It's best to plant them closer rather than farther apart, because this will reduce any necessary weeding.

To weed around your carrots, use a hoe and do it carefully so as not to disturb the foliage. Water if the soil is particularly dry, but take care not to overwater. Try to keep the soil moisture consistent, because a sudden watering or downpour on dry soil can cause the carrots to split.

SEEING IN THE DARK

It is true that carrots help you see in the dark. Your liver converts the betacarotene into vitamin A, which in turn makes a pigment in the retina that you need for night vision. Eating carrots also protects against macular degeneration, the major cause of vision loss in later life.

WHY EAT CARROTS?

BETACAROTENE Carrots are one of the best sources of this vital natural chemical, which your body converts into vitamin A.

VITAMINS C AND K They are also an excellent source of these two vitamins, an average serving providing a fifth of your daily needs.

FIBRE Good source.

HARVESTING AND STORING

The only carrots suitable for storing are maincrop. Early varieties, even if they are planted later for autumn or early winter harvesting, won't store well. The best way to store your carrots is to leave them in the ground with enough protection to withstand light frosts. However, to avoid muddy boots and frozen fingers, I pull mine, or lift them with a fork, when they're ready, and store them in old wooden wine boxes between layers of sharp sand.

HOW TO COOK

Carrots are delicious eaten raw with dips and in salads, or juiced with apple and celery. However, the betacarotene they contain is more easily absorbed by the body when they're cooked. Don't overcook them, though, or you'll lose other nutrients.

Make them into soup. Steam or boil them, or add to stews, casseroles and stir-fries. One of my favourite ways of cooking them is to roast them in goose fat with potatoes and the Sunday joint. Whatever you do with carrots, they add flavour, sweetness and an enormous nutritional boost to any dish.

To freeze them, cut into slices or julienne strips, blanch in boiling water for one minute, refresh in ice-cold water and freeze in bags. Otherwise freeze them as soup and in finished dishes.

WARNING!

Commercially produced carrots often contain high residues of pesticides, so if not organic, they should be peeled, topped and tailed. This is especially important if you're making purée for babies or small children, because the pesticides are most concentrated in the tops and bottoms. Carrots are always best from your own garden or an organic supplier – these need just washing and brushing.

Potatoes

Everyone should eat potatoes because they're delicious, nutritious and absolutely *not fattening* – 100g (3½oz) of boiled potatoes has only 80 calories; the same amount of roast spuds contains 157. Cook them as chips and the calorie count goes up to almost 300, while for crisps it's a whopping 533. It's obvious that how you cook potatoes makes the difference.

Potatoes are rich in nutrients, which is just as well as around half of the total vitamin C intake in the British diet is supplied by this amazing tuber– which doesn't say much for the UK consumption of other veg or fruit! The skin and flesh together make the humble spud as valuable as brassicas in terms of cancer protection. Red-skinned potatoes have the strongest antioxidants.

Varieties are split into first and second crop earlies (summer's 'new' potatoes) and maincrop. First earlies are usually ready to harvest within three months of planting. Second earlies take a few weeks longer. Maincrop potatoes are ready in four months, but can be left in the ground for longer.

Cultivation

Choose a light, sunny position, with well-drained soil. When preparing the site the previous autumn, add plenty of well-rotted manure. Before planting, in early to late spring, rake up any large clods of soil. Dig a trench and plant each potato so that most of the chittings are pointing upwards. Take care not to break off any of the shoots. Earlies should be planted 15cm (6in) deep, 30cm (12in) apart with 60cm (24in) between rows; plant maincrop 40–75cm (16–30in) apart.

Plants take four to eight weeks to germinate. As soon as shoots start to show, the potatoes will need earthing up to protect them from frost and light. Break up the soil in between the rows with a fork or hoe and draw up a pile of the loose soil against the stems to produce a ridge. Repeat every week so that the potatoes don't reach the surface (if exposed to light, they will become green and poisonous). Water well, especially during early growth.

To avoid risk of soil contamination, don't grow potatoes on the same plot as the previous year.

When preparing potatoes, don't wash, peel or cut them until just before cooking, because they start to oxidize and lose vitamin C immediately.

Chitting

The easiest option is to grow potatoes from seed potatoes. Buy them four to eight weeks before planting and set them with their 'eyes' upwards, either in egg boxes or seed trays.

Place the seed potatoes in a light, cool position and wait for short, green shoots, known as chittings, to develop. Egg boxes are ideal.

Each chitted potato needs two or three sprouts, so rub off any extra. Lay sprouted ends upwards on potting compost, and cover with a 15-cm (6-in) layer of compost.

When leaves appear, cover with more compost and water regularly. Continue 'earthing up' for several weeks. Harvest once they have flowered.

WHY EAT POTATOES?

VITAMIN C Excellent source.
VITAMIN B6 Good source.
FIBRE Good source.
PHYTONUTRIENTS Potatoes contain a significant amount of several phytonutrients known for their protective antioxidant benefits.
PROTEIN Potatoes contain a small amount of protein, including a special group that protects them during storage and appears to have powerful antioxidant properties.
POTASSIUM The skin of potatoes, especially, is rich in this mineral.

HARVESTING AND STORING

Early potatoes are normally ready in early summer, but they can also be planted in midsummer for late autumn harvesting. Lift them and eat as required because they don't store well. I love planting new potatoes in a plastic dustbin in the greenhouse in early autumn so they are ready to eat with cold turkey the day after Christmas.

It's best to harvest maincrop potatoes as needed, but if you're going to store some over winter, leave them in the ground for as long as possible, until the winter weather sets in. Bear in mind, though, that there is a greater chance of slugs getting to them. Try to collect them on a dry day, and don't wash or clean them. Store in hessian or paper sacks in a cool, dark, dry and frost-free place. They also keep well in wooden crates between layers of sandy soil or a peat substitute.

WARNING!
Never keep potatoes in plastic or plastic-lined sacks because they will sweat and rot. When using stored potatoes, cut out any green parts that may develop – these contain solanine, a poisonous chemical.

HOW TO COOK

The healthiest way to cook potatoes is without fat, so boiling, steaming or baking are ideal. If you must eat chips – and there's nothing wrong with them occasionally – remember that thick chips soak up far less fat than skinny ones.

Peeling potatoes is very wasteful because the skin is rich in potassium, fibre, vitamin C and protein. However, like all root veg, commercial produce is likely to contain pesticide residues. That's why growing your own or buying organic is best.

Jerusalem artichokes

The strange knobbly appearance of this nutritious tuber seems to put people off, which is a shame because it's easy to grow, wonderful to cook and as versatile as a potato. Plant in late winter to early spring for a fabulous harvest throughout the following autumn and winter.

Jerusalem artichokes were first brought to Europe from their native Canada by the French in 1605. In fact, they are native to most of North America, and these artichokes were important to the Native American from whom the settlers learnt about their value and versatility.

No relation to the globe artichoke, although the two have a similar flavour and nutritional composition, Jerusalem artichokes are from the same family as sunflowers – their Latin name is *Helianthus tuberosus*. The Italians call them *girasol* (a species of sunflower) and it's generally believed they acquired the name Jerusalem as a corruption of the Italian, which the English couldn't pronounce. They were brought to England by the Dutch and by the 1800s were being used to make a popular soup that went by the name of Palestine soup since it was believed they actually came from Jerusalem.

Whether roasted, fried or sautéed, or used raw or in soups, they are nutritionally extremely interesting. They are low in salt and calories, containing 78 per 100g (3½oz), and they contain a substance known as inulin. The body deals with this in the same way as fibre, which means it isn't broken down during normal digestion but ends up in the large bowel (colon) where it provides food for billions of friendly bacteria. The resulting fermentation can

One of the newer varieties that I've found is Fuseau. It's a heavy cropper with reasonably smooth tubers, making it easier to peel if you want to. It should be available from good garden centres or specialist suppliers.

sometimes be a cause of wind, but that's a small price to pay for the fabulous taste and the low glycaemic index (GI) benefits of this much underrated vegetable.

Cultivation

These perennials will grow almost anywhere and in most soils. Once established, they tend to take over, so you'll need a well-contained area. Fortunately, they do well in a very large pot or half barrel, which may be the answer if you have a small garden.

Plant any time between late winter and mid-spring. For decent-sized tubers, plant thinly 15cm (6in) deep and 30cm (12in) apart with 75cm (30in) between rows. The plants grow tall and straight, reaching about 3 metres (10ft), with rich green leaves. They make a perfect windbreak for a vegetable plot, but they also block the

SPECIAL DIETS

• Although rich in carbohydrates, Jerusalem artichokes contain very little sugar, making them ideal for diabetics and anyone who has problems keeping their blood sugar levels on an even keel.

• Dried and ground into flour, they are perfect for anyone with gluten, wheat or other cereal allergies.

WHY EAT JERUSALEM ARTICHOKES?

INULIN A wonderful natural source of this substance, which improves digestion and sustains the billions of friendly bugs in your gut.
MINERALS An excellent source of potassium and a good source of iron, copper, thiamin and phosphorus.
VITAMINS A useful source of B vitamins.

STORING AND COOKING

Jerusalem artichokes are best stored in the ground where they grow. Lift as needed and cook as soon as possible. For most recipes, there's no point peeling Jerusalem artichokes. It's very wasteful and time-consuming, and you lose a lot of the nutrients. All you need is a good stiff vegetable brush and plenty of running water to get them perfectly clean. Remove any whiskery side roots, top and tail the tubers and they're ready to use. They are the perfect accompaniment to roast pheasant or pheasant casserole – probably because these game birds love to eat them.

sun, so take care where you put them. I've even seen a maze planted with Jerusalem artichokes. They are amazingly immune to pests, but rabbits and pheasants will have a peck at them.

Most gardening books tell you they won't often flower in the UK. That may be true in the north, but where I used to live in the Chilterns they produce stunning bright yellow flowers like miniature sunflowers. When they've grown to about 30cm (12in), it's worth pulling a little earth up the stems

to prevent wind damage and protect the tubers from sunlight. Other than that, there's not much to do. The dense foliage prevents any serious weed growth but they will need some water if you have a very dry spell.

As the leaves start to die back (late autumn/early winter), cut the stems down to about 7.5cm (3in). I normally lay the cut stems over the bed as frost protection. The tubers are extremely hardy and unless you have a major slug problem they'll keep much better in the soil than in storage. They're usually perfect to eat from mid-autumn onwards and I've used mine well into spring.

You'll never lift all of them, so the next year they'll come up by themselves. My bed is in its fifth year and all I do is thin out the clumps of stems when they get too thick, put on a good layer of well-rotted compost in the spring and give them one feed with liquid seaweed – minimum effort, maximum return, and a joy to look at in the summer.

EXTRA SUPPORT

As the plants get bigger, high early autumn winds can damage them, so I put stakes at each end of the rows and one on each side at the middle, and just run a string all the way round at a height of about 1 metre (3ft), for added support.

Beetroot

For centuries, folklore and traditional medicine have been enough to recommend the advantages of eating beetroot. Everyone would benefit from having a good portion every week, and the beauty of growing it yourself is that you get to eat the hugely nutritious leaves as well as the root.

Beetroot is thought to have evolved from sea beet a few thousand years ago. It was first cultivated for its medicinal properties, although in ancient Greek history it is referred to as a food of the gods, and the Romans seem to have enjoyed it for its taste as well. Eventually, from around the eighteenth century onwards, it became very popular, particularly in eastern Europe from where the famous beetroot soup, borscht, originates.

An excellent energy booster, beetroot is great for athletes because it increases the amount of oxygen that cells can absorb by up to 400 per cent, and it's low in calories. It's also a good food for convalescents, providing added strength and resistance, and as a blood builder to help combat anaemia and other blood disorders.

The red pigments give beetroot its heart-protective and anti-cancer function, and make it a strongly anti-inflammatory food. However, these pigments also cause beeturia, a condition that produces red urine in some people. Don't worry – you're not having a haemorrhage.

Cultivation

Beetroot likes a neutral soil with neither too much lime nor too much acid; and the earth needs to be fairly soft, without

Beetroot seeds have a corky texture and can be slow to germinate. Ideally, soak them in warm water overnight just before planting to help them along, and don't sow them in cold ground.

too much clay or sand. Choose an open, sunny position and mulch the site well before planting.

Sow beetroot seeds 2cm (¾in) deep, 5 to 10cm (2 to 4in) apart, in short rows; and sow every 14 days from early spring to late summer for a continuous crop. There's no need to thin out the seedlings. Each seed produces three or four roots, which don't develop at the same rate. The dominant one can be picked first, allowing the others to grow on.

Weed by hand, or hoe carefully between the rows. Try not to scuff the plant with the hoe or trowel because the roots can bleed. Water every day until the leaves start to sprout. In the absence of rain, continue to water every few days. Once the leaves have become established, the root system will gather its own moisture from the soil. In dry spells, water established plants every 10 to 14 days. Don't overwater or the plant will produce fine leaves but a poor root. Lack of water will produce woody roots.

WHY EAT BEETROOT?

VITAMIN K The leaves contain vast amounts of this important vitamin.

VITAMIN A The leaves also contain huge amounts of vitamin A.

VITAMIN C The leaves are an excellent source of vitamin C. The root contains a small amount.

CAROTENOIDS The leaves are hugely rich in lutein and zeaxanthin, the two carotenoids that protect the eyes from macular degeneration.

FOLATE The root is a good source of this important vitamin (B9), which is necessary for the formation of blood cells and helps in the prevention of anaemia.

MINERALS The root and leaves contain manganese and potassium as well as small amounts of other minerals.

FIBRE The root is a useful source of fibre.

HARVESTING AND STORING

You will be able to see enough of the root to give you an idea of how big it is. Harvest when the beetroots are about the size of a small orange. Don't let them grow too large because they'll lose some of their flavour. They can be left in the ground until autumn, but if left too long they will develop a woody texture.

You can store beetroots in layers of sharp sand in wooden boxes and they'll keep for several months in a frost-free, dry environment – but keep the mice out. Both the greens and the roots will freeze after cooking, but not when raw.

HOW TO COOK

Steam the roots until they're soft enough just to pierce with a fork, boil in the minimum amount of water or bake baby beets and serve with a white sauce. Don't overcook because too much heat will destroy the phytonutrients as well as the B and C vitamins – grated raw as a salad with a light dressing of olive oil and lemon juice is the best way to retain all the nutrients.

To cook beetroot greens, wash them well, leave wet and cook for a minute or two in a saucepan – just like spinach.

Parsnips

The Romans knew a thing or two about good food and planted magnificent kitchen gardens by their villas. One of their prized vegetables was the parsnip, and wild parsnip has been used for centuries in Europe and the UK. However, the cultivated parsnip as we now know it didn't appear until the Middle Ages.

Parnsips were once a staple of the European diet, popular for their sweetness and their nutty flavour, but that changed once the potato became established. Now, I'm pleased to say, this much denigrated vegetable is in demand once again, perhaps thanks to its inclusion in many dishes by contemporary chefs.

These vegetables are best eaten in winter. For optimum flavour, parsnips need to be frosted in the ground. I think the forced, artificially fed, out-of-season crops are bland and probably less good for you than the winter crop at its best. Parsnips are virtually free of fat, cholesterol and salt, and although not hugely rich in nutrients, a decent portion has valuable amounts of your daily nutritional requirements. They are hardy plants and need little attention while they're growing.

Cultivation

Deep, sandy, fertile and stone-free soil is best, although there are short, stubby varieties of parsnip that will grow in stony soil, as well as in deep pots on the patio. Generally, they like sun or light shade – they are unlikely to germinate in the cold – and prefer soil that has had some well-rotted manure dug in, and has a fine texture. Avoid using fresh manure.

If you leave a few unharvested roots in the ground, their spring flowers will attract beneficial predators, such as hoverflies, which eat aphids and other destructive insects.

Sow seeds from late winter to mid-spring directly into the ground in drills 2cm (¾in) deep and 20 to 25cm (8 to 10in) apart. Drop in three or four seeds at 13 to 15cm (5 to 6in) intervals, and water generously with a fine spray. When the seedlings are large enough to handle, and if they're looking too crowded, pinch out a few, leaving the strongest plants.

Hoe your parsnip crop regularly to keep down weeds, taking care not to touch the crowns of the growing plants. They like moist soil, so water during dry spells – little and often to keep the moisture levels even.

> **TIP**
>
> I always put an empty plastic bottle on top of each marker cane when the leaves are dying off – why risk an eye injury? The noise of the bottles in the wind keeps birds away from other crops, and the vibration in the soil frightens off moles and mice, which might otherwise nibble at the roots.

WHY EAT PARSNIPS?

VITAMIN C Valuable source.
FOLIC ACID Good source.
FIBRE Good source.
MINERALS Useful amounts of potassium and copper.
VITAMIN E Parsnips have some vitamin E, which is important for heart protection and to boost circulation.

HARVESTING AND STORING

Parsnips are best left in the ground and dug up as required. They're easier to harvest if you mulch around them with a good layer of straw, so the soil doesn't freeze too solidly. Before the leaves die off completely, it's a good idea to mark each root with a cane in case you lose them in the snow.

If you do want to store them, put them between layers of sharp sand in sturdy boxes, but don't let them touch each other. For short-term use, they'll keep in a plastic bag in the refrigerator for up to two weeks.

HOW TO COOK

Parsnips are delicious, and retain most of their nutrients, when brushed with oil and roasted until crisp on the outside and fondant in the middle. Boiled and puréed on their own with a little nutmeg, or combined with carrots, swedes, potatoes or celeriac, their delicate flavour is a perfect accompaniment to any grilled or roast meat, poultry or fish.

Radishes

Most people eat radishes because they taste good. The French eat them with butter and salt, which tastes good but isn't exactly healthy. What makes them healthy is the fact that they're part of the Cruciferae family – just like cabbage and all its relatives. For this reason, they provide glucosinolates and other sulphurous compounds that protect against cancer.

Radishes don't contain huge amounts of conventional nutrients, but have been a long-time favourite of herbalists, who use them for the treatment of liver and gall bladder problems. They stimulate the gall bladder, increasing the flow of bile into the stomach, making it easier to digest fatty food (so perhaps the French have got it right!).

Radishes were first eaten in Europe in pre-Roman times, and in the early nineteenth century, a black radish was common in England and France. Now the round or tubular red, pink or white crunchy radishes are most familiar. They come in summer and winter varieties, and regular sowing of a good selection means you can eat home-grown radishes for most of the year, even with an unheated greenhouse. They are a great crop

Use a 'mixed radish' seed, so that the plants will mature at different times – and don't sow too many at a time because they're very quick to grow and will easily go to seed if they're not eaten.

for filling spaces between rows of carrots and peas, or intercropping with slow-growing plants, such as parsnips or onions.

Cultivation

Radishes thrive in most soils, but they prefer well-drained and stone-free ground. They like a sunny spot for spring sowing, but need some shade for summer sowing – another reason to grow them between other vegetables that can offer a little protection.

Sow summer varieties outdoors in early spring, or under cloches in late winter. Sow winter varieties in late summer for harvesting from late autumn onwards. Rake the soil to create a fine surface, remove any stones and sow seed thinly, 1cm (½in) deep, in drills. Rows of summer radishes should be 15cm (6in) apart; winter radishes 30cm (12in) apart. If seedlings look overcrowded, pinch some out, leaving the stronger plants. Thin small varieties to 2.5cm (1in) intervals, and large varieties to 5 to 10cm (24in) intervals. Hoe regularly in order to keep weeds under control.

WARNING!

Some varieties of radish can be very hot and peppery. If you have a stomach ulcer or any inflammatory digestive disorder, eat with caution. Radishes are also goitreogenic, which means they interfere with the uptake of iodine, so shouldn't be eaten by anyone with an underactive thyroid or using thyroxin replacement medication.

WHY EAT RADISHES?

GLUCOSINOLATES Radishes are a good source of these and other sulphurous compounds, which protect against cancer.
VITAMIN C Good source.
FOLATE They contain a small amount of this vitamin (B9).
FIBRE Small amount.
POTASSIUM Small amount.

HARVESTING AND STORING

Harvest radishes frequently to prevent them from getting large and woody. Certainly don't let them go to seed. Once picked, they're best eaten as quickly as possible, although they will keep for a few days in a closed plastic bag in the salad drawer of the fridge.

HOW TO COOK

Radishes are best eaten raw and as fresh as possible, when they're still young and crisp. The green tops are also nutritious and tasty and can be puréed with some cooked carrot or potato to make a dip.

Beetroot, cabbage and onion soup with cider vinegar

The combination of two renowned healing vegetables, cabbage and beetroot, with the prince of folk medicines, cider vinegar, makes this traditional Polish peasant soup a triumph of goodness as well as flavour. It's perfect for children, athletes, academics, pregnant women and anyone recovering from an illness. Served with salad and wholemeal bread, it makes an excellent lunch or supper.

BENEFITS

- Rich in vitamin C and antibacterial sulphur.
- Full of plant chemicals that protect against cancer.
- This soup boosts the immune system as well as being fatigue-fighting and blood-building.

Serves 4

1 medium onion, finely chopped

1 clove garlic, finely chopped

2 tbsp olive oil

450g (1lb) raw beetroot, diced

1 litre (1¾ pints) vegetable stock

2 tbsp cider vinegar

½ red or green or white cabbage, shredded

swirl of cream, yogurt or crème fraîche (optional)

8 whole chives

Sweat the onion and garlic in the oil for 5 minutes. Add the beetroot and stir for 2 minutes. Pour in the stock and simmer until the vegetables are tender. Add the cider vinegar, cool a little, then liquidize until smooth.

Return the soup to the pan, scatter the cabbage on top, cover and simmer gently for 5 minutes, until the cabbage is cooked but crunchy. Add a swirl of cream, yogurt or crème fraîche first, if you like. Serve with 2 chives arranged on top of each bowl.

Timbale of beetroot

In this substantial salad, the crunchy sweetness of carrot mixes with the heat of the radish and the unmistakable flavour of celeriac. Extra iron from the raisins and the blood-building red pigments in beetroot make this especially good if you are recovering from an illness or operation. It looks fantastic and is easier to make than you might think. Serve it with a fish or meat dish, hot or cold, or surrounded by slices of hard-boiled egg.

BENEFITS

- Beetroot is a rich source of fibre, carbohydrates and vitamin B.

Serves 4

1 large carrot

1 bunch of radishes

½ a celeriac

2 medium beetroots, cooked

400g (14oz) basmati rice, cooked

2 tbsp flat-leaf parsley, finely chopped

1 tbsp chives, finely snipped

110g (4oz) raisins

30ml (2 tbsp) extra virgin olive oil

8 whole chives

Trim, peel and grate the vegetables, and mix thoroughly with the cooked rice. Add the chopped herbs, raisins and olive oil and again mix thoroughly. Firmly press the mixture into timbale pots and put them in the fridge for at least an hour before turning out. Decorate with the whole chives.

TIP: A timbale pot is a fairly deep, straight-sided tin, usually either round or oval in shape. I find that lightly oiling the inside of the pots works well, and using a flat, round pusher to tamp down the mixture. You can buy pots and pushers in kitchen shops and good supermarkets.

Beetroot, orange, radish and walnut salad

Ancient Greeks revered beetroot as a medicine and offered it as a tribute to Apollo in the temple at Delphi. Now herbalists recommend it, and plenty of folklore supports its reputation. Although there's not yet a great deal of scientific evidence for its medicinal value, research has found that drinking beetroot juice can help to lower high blood pressure and reduce the life-threatening risks of this condition.

Serves 4

4 medium-sized cooked beetroots, cubed

500ml (18fl oz) fresh orange juice

zest of 1 orange, plus orange slices to garnish

5 tbsp olive oil

75g (3oz) shelled walnuts

10 radishes, washed and thinly sliced

Put the beetroot, orange juice, zest and olive oil in a pan and simmer gently for 10 minutes. Increase the heat and boil until most of the liquid has evaporated.

Meanwhile, dry-fry the walnuts until they are just turning brown, about 2 minutes.

Serve the beetroot in its juice, scattered with the walnuts and radishes.

TIP: Beetroot can stain hands and plastics, so wear gloves and use glass or stainless steel bowls and saucepans.

BENEFITS

- Beetroot contains blood-enhancing nutrients.
- Walnuts are rich in protein and minerals.
- Radishes add extra cancer-protective and liver-stimulating plant chemicals.

Steamed halibut with turnips, parsnips and potatoes

Halibut is a fabulous fish, both in taste and texture, and also exceptionally healthy since it's low in fat and sodium. When you take account of the root vegetables, this becomes an outstanding Superfoods meal.

BENEFITS

- Halibut is full of protein – each portion of this dish contains a day's worth.
- Each portion also contains more than your daily requirement of selenium.
- Halibut is a good source of vitamins B6 and B12, and of the minerals magnesium and potassium.

Serves 4

4 halibut fillets, about 4cm (1½in) thick

4 sprigs fresh dill

1 medium onion, quartered

1 bottle white wine

225g (8oz) each of turnips, parsnips and potatoes, peeled and diced

2 cloves garlic, finely chopped

25g (1oz) unsalted butter

sea salt and freshly ground black pepper

Season the fish on both sides, put into a steamer basket, sprinkle with the dill and set aside. Put the onion and wine into a saucepan that will hold the steamer basket. Boil for 2 minutes, add the root vegetables and garlic and boil for a further 2 minutes.

Place the steamer basket over the pan, cover tightly and steam for 8 minutes until the fish is opaque. Remove and keep warm.

Discard the onion and, using a slotted spoon, transfer the rest of the vegetables into a bowl, dot with the butter and keep warm.

Return the pan to the heat and boil until the liquid is reduced to about 100ml (3½fl oz).

Divide the vegetables between 4 plates, put a halibut fillet on top of each one, pour on some sauce and serve.

TIP: It is important not to overcook the fish, so keep an eye on it and don't forget that it will carry on cooking after you take it out of the steamer. Make sure it's just opaque and don't let it get solid white because it will then be dry and tough instead of moist and as soft as butter.

SO DIGESTIBLE!

The starch in cooked potatoes is easily digested, making them a good food for invalids, anyone with digestive problems and an excellent weaning food for babies.

Jerusalem artichoke and leek soup

Nothing could be simpler or more delicious than this soup whether you eat it hot or cold. To make it more substantial, or turn it into a smart dinner party starter, add some mussels.

Serves 4

1 medium onion, chopped

small knob of butter

2 tbsp virgin olive oil

1 leek, washed and chopped

1 clove garlic, finely chopped

700g (1½lb) Jerusalem artichokes, scrubbed and cut into 1cm (½in) slices

2 bay leaves

1.2 litres (2 pints) vegetable stock

a little warm milk (optional)

4–5 mussels per person (optional)

freshly ground black pepper

chives, finely snipped, to garnish

parsley, finely chopped

Sweat the onions in butter and oil until they are just soft. Add the leek and garlic, and stir gently for 2 minutes. Add the artichokes, stirring for a further 2 minutes. Season with black pepper. Add the bay leaves and stock, bring to the boil and simmer gently until all the vegetables are soft – around 10 minutes. Allow to cool a little before liquidizing. The soup should be fairly thick but if necessary thin it by stirring in a little warm milk.

If you are adding mussels, make sure they're all tightly closed and throw out any that don't close up when tapped on the worktop. Wash thoroughly in a sieve under running water and put them into a large, flat-bottomed saucepan. Turn up the heat and cover. Within 5 minutes the shells will open and the mussels will be cooked. Throw out any that haven't opened.

Pour the soup into four bowls, put the mussels (if using) on top and sprinkle with the chives and parsley.

Beetroot risotto

Beetroot is a strengthening vegetable, and one of the most important foods of Romany traditional medicine. A good source of both instant and slow-release energy, this recipe is perfect for anyone recovering from extreme physical exertion or illness.

Serves 4

1 large onion, thinly sliced

75g (3oz) unsalted butter

450g (1lb) cooked beetroot, peeled and diced

450g (1lb) arborio – or, better still, carnaroli – rice

75ml (3fl oz) dry white wine

1.2 litres (2 pints) vegetable stock

small handful chives, finely snipped

small handful flat-leaf parsley, finely chopped

60g (2oz) Parmesan cheese, freshly grated

Fry the onion gently in half the butter, until soft but not coloured. Add the beetroot and cook for a few minutes until it starts to soften. Add the rice and stir until the grains are all coated with the butter. Pour in the wine and boil rapidly for a minute or two to reduce it.

Add the hot stock a ladleful at a time, stirring until the rice has absorbed it. Continue until all the stock is used and the rice still has some crunch – about 25 minutes. Stir in the remaining butter, the herbs and the Parmesan.

Leave to stand, covered, for 2 minutes to enhance the flavours before serving.

Jerusalem artichoke salad

Few people eat raw Jerusalem artichokes, which is a shame because they taste wonderful. You will need a very sharp knife and a good grater.

BENEFITS

- This recipe is real 'rainbow eating', providing massive amounts of protective antioxidant plant chemicals that help ward off wrinkles, heart disease and some forms of cancer.

Serves 4

450g (1lb) Jerusalem artichokes, scrubbed and coarsely grated

½ small red cabbage, sliced very thinly and roughly chopped

½ small white cabbage, sliced very thinly and roughly chopped

4 medium carrots, scrubbed and cut into batons

4 handfuls watercress, thoroughly washed and dried

4 tbsp walnuts, roughly chopped

juice of 1 lemon

walnut oil

Arrange the vegetables in piles around the outside of each plate with a handful of watercress in the middle. Sprinkle with walnuts and drizzle with lemon juice (not on the artichokes) and walnut oil.

TIP: Once you cut or chop Jerusalem artichokes, they go brown. To prevent this, put the grated artichoke into a bowl, sprinkle with a little lemon juice and mix thoroughly.

Braised pheasant on a bed of Jerusalem artichokes

The local pheasants appear to like our garden. Lots of them are to be seen strutting about there during the season and I often see them hiding in the huge thicket of growing Jerusalem artichokes. They seem to be the only creatures that like to peck at the leaves and roots. Pheasants and artichokes taste good when they're cooked together, with the artichokes soaking up all the wonderful juices from the pheasant.

BENEFITS

- Pheasant is rich in iron and low in fat.
- Jerusalem artichokes have plenty of fibre to help reduce cholesterol, making this a heart, digestion and blood-friendly dish.

Serves 2

110g (4oz) unsalted butter

1 pheasant, cleaned

450g (1lb) Jerusalem artichokes, scrubbed and cut into 1cm (½in) slices

400ml (14fl oz) dry white wine

freshly ground black pepper

Preheat the oven to 190°C/375°F/gas 5.

In a large ovenproof casserole dish, melt the butter on top of the stove and sauté the pheasant, turning regularly until it's brown all over. Remove the bird, put the artichokes in the casserole dish and add the white wine and plenty of black pepper. Put the pheasant back in the pot on top of the artichokes and cover the bird with buttered greaseproof paper. Put the lid on the casserole and cook in the oven for 50 minutes. Then remove the lid and greaseproof paper and cook for another 10 minutes to brown the pheasant breasts.

Serve the bird on a large platter surrounded by the artichokes.

Lamb and root veg pie

Traditionally made with mutton, which is not easy to find today, this recipe is just as good using very lean lamb. My wife's mother, Patsy, introduced me to it. Sally and I first met in London and it was the most amazing coincidence when we discovered that her mother lived in the very next village to me, in rural Hertfordshire. You can make the filling two or three days in advance. Reheat it when ready, put on the pastry lid and you'll be eating it in under half an hour. I sometimes make it in earthenware, ovenproof dishes, one for each person.

Serves 6

4 tbsp rapeseed oil

1kg (2¼lb) lamb with all fat removed, cubed

bowl of well-seasoned plain flour

1 large onion, chopped

2 cloves garlic, finely chopped

2 sticks celery with leaves, finely chopped

1 parsnip, peeled and cubed

1 turnip, peeled and cubed

½ swede, peeled and cubed

1 leek, washed and sliced diagonally

2 large carrots, peeled, halved and sliced

1 large glass red wine

3 bay leaves

1 bouquet garni

1 tbsp tomato purée

1 litre (1¾ pints) vegetable stock (preferably home-made)

1 packet ready-made puff pastry

1 free-range egg, beaten

In a large, heavy saucepan, heat the oil. Coat the meat in the flour and add to the pan, stirring constantly until the lamb is browned all over.

Remove the pan from the heat, take out the lamb and add the onion, garlic and celery, and a little more oil if needed. Keep stirring until the vegetables are soft but not brown.

Add all the remaining vegetables and stir until they are coated with oil. Return the meat to the pan and stir for a minute or two. Add the red wine, bay leaves, bouquet garni and tomato purée and stir until bubbling.

Add the stock, cover and simmer until the meat and vegetables are tender, approximately 1–1½ hours.

Preheat the oven to 200°C/400°F/gas 6. Roll out the pastry to a size that's big enough to cover your pie dish with a good overhang all round. Put the filling into the dish and, if necessary, put a pie funnel or an upturned egg cup in the middle to support the pastry.

Lay the pastry over the dish and cut around the outside. Use a fork to crimp the edge all round. Brush with the beaten egg and place in the middle of the oven for 20–30 minutes until the pastry is golden and crisp.

BENEFITS

■ This dish contains plenty of fibre, masses of protein and very little fat, and is hugely satisfying.

■ Slow-release energy comes from the fibre and complex sugars in the root vegetables, which are rich in vitamins and minerals.

■ One portion contains a day's betacarotene (for vitamin A).

■ Onions, leeks and garlic provide antioxidants.

Gratin of parsnips, potatoes and sweet potatoes

Like so many vegetable dishes, this is best eaten warm rather than piping hot. The Italians seldom serve overheated vegetables, because you lose so much of the flavour. This recipe is just as good cold with salads or cold meats.

BENEFITS

- Parsnips are a good source of potassium, and a super source of fibre, vitamin C and folic acid. Potassium helps prevent heart disease as well as cramp.
- Sweet potatoes are even richer in fibre, and also contain a huge amount of betacarotene, which your body converts into vitamin A.

Serves 4

400g (14oz) parsnips, peeled and halved – or quartered lengthwise, depending on thickness

400g (14oz) potatoes, cut into 1cm (½in) slices

400g (14oz) sweet potatoes cut into 1cm (½in) slices

75g (3oz) unsalted butter

50g (2oz) flour

600ml (1 pint) milk

1 tsp organic savoury seasoning

110g (4oz) Gruyère or Emmenthal cheese, grated

Preheat the oven to 200°C/400°F/gas 6.

Parboil the vegetables until they are just tender – about 10 minutes – and arrange in an ovenproof dish.

Melt the butter in a large saucepan and stir in the flour. Keep stirring until the mixture thickens – about 2 minutes – and then gradually add the milk and savoury seasoning, still stirring constantly. Cook for 5 minutes. Pour the sauce over the vegetables, sprinkle with the cheese and bake for 15 minutes until golden brown.

Jerusalem artichoke dauphinoise

This is a great supper dish for four hungry people, served with a simple green salad and crusty wholemeal bread, and any leftovers are just as good cold. It also makes a wonderful side dish for six, served with duck, beef, lamb or venison. It's worth peeling the artichokes for this dish because they look better without the brown skin.

BENEFITS

- Jerusalem artichokes improve digestion and boost natural resistance, while thyme protects against infections.
- Onions and garlic protect the heart (offset by the cream and butter, but a little of what you fancy!)

Serves 4

juice of ½ lemon

900g (2lb) Jerusalem artichokes, peeled and cut into chunks

6 thin rashers pancetta

small knob of butter

2 tbsp olive oil

2 medium onions, thinly sliced

3 cloves garlic, finely chopped

1 tbsp fresh thyme, leaves only

300ml (10fl oz) dry white wine

300ml (10fl oz) vegetable stock

200ml (7fl oz) double cream

Preheat the oven to 200°C/400°F/gas 6.

Fill a bowl with cold water, add the lemon juice and put the chopped artichokes straight into the water to prevent browning. Cook the pancetta on a griddle pan without fat (or put under the grill) until crispy and leave to cool.

Heat the butter and oil in a medium-sized saucepan and sweat the onions for 2–3 minutes before adding the garlic and thyme. Cook gently for another 5 minutes. Add the artichokes and stir to coat thoroughly with the oil for another 2 minutes. Add the wine and stock, bring to the boil and simmer for 10 minutes. Remove from the heat, crumble the pancetta and stir in with the cream.

Pour the mixture into an ovenproof dish and cook in the oven for 10 minutes. Reduce the heat to 190°C/375°F/gas 5 for another 45 minutes or until the dauphinoise is brown and bubbling.

Warm spinach and Jerusalem artichoke salad

Among my favourite recipes are many that I've collected from my patients, and some of the best come from a group of Italian mothers and grannies I've been looking after for several decades. I particularly love the Italian way with vegetables and salads – they never serve them ice cold and tasteless, or boiling hot and mouth-burning. This one is a wonderful mixture of textures and flavours, and makes an unusual and intriguing accompaniment to chicken or fish dishes. It's perfect with grilled or baked cod, hake, halibut and salmon steaks.

BENEFITS

- Bursting with health-giving nutrients.

Serves 4

225g (8oz) Jerusalem artichokes, scrubbed, topped and tailed

85g (3oz) butter

450g (1lb) large-leaf spinach, thoroughly washed and left wet

extra virgin olive oil

nutmeg

Put the artichokes in a saucepan and just cover with cold water. Add 25g (1oz) of butter, bring to the boil and simmer uncovered until the water has boiled away – 5–10 minutes depending on how fresh the artichokes are.

While the artichokes are cooking, pile the damp spinach into a large saucepan, cover and cook on a moderate heat until wilted – 3–4 minutes. Strain any surplus water, return the spinach to the saucepan, add the rest of the butter and chop coarsely with a sharp knife. Sprinkle with freshly ground nutmeg.

Pile the spinach in the centre of a warmed serving dish, arrange the artichokes around the outside and drizzle with a little olive oil.

Rabbit parcels with three purées

I have fought many battles over rabbit recipes, mostly with people who grew up on *Peter Rabbit* or *Watership Down*. They may munch cheerfully on baby lamb, roast duck or veal chops, but have a fit at the thought of eating a rabbit, despite rabbits being verminous creatures that eat their way through your vegetable garden. That's what makes them so healthy and tasty, of course. However, if you prefer, you can substitute chicken breasts for the rabbit legs in this recipe and you still have a plateful of Superfoods, mostly from your own garden.

BENEFITS

- Rabbit is very rich in protein – one portion of this dish has a day's worth.
- Rabbit contains just about the lowest amount of fat of any meat.
- The vegetables contain huge amounts of betacarotene, vitamin C and antioxidant chemicals.

Serves 4

4 rabbit legs

1 shallot, finely chopped

450g (1lb) broccoli, four of the florets removed

450g (1lb) carrots, peeled and about a quarter of them sliced into fine strips

450g (1lb) potatoes, peeled and about a quarter of them sliced into fine strips

4 pinches fennel seeds

2 sticks of lemongrass cut into 4 2.5cm (1in) sticks

200ml (7fl oz) carrot juice

275g (10oz) unsalted butter

60ml (4 tbsp) crème fraîche

Preheat the oven to 200°C/400°F/gas 6.

Cut four squares of kitchen foil big enough to envelop the rabbit legs very loosely. Divide the shallot, broccoli florets and strips of carrot and potato between the foil squares and top with the rabbit legs. Season and sprinkle with the fennel seeds and lemongrass. Carefully divide the carrot juice between the parcels, seal and put into the oven for 35 minutes.

Meanwhile, cook the rest of the potatoes, carrots and broccoli separately. Put them through a processor, again separately, divide the butter and crème fraîche between them, mix well and keep warm.

Serve the parcels, closed, on individual plates, with mounds of purée arranged around them.

TIP: Despite the vast selection of electric mixers, processors, liquidizers and other gadgets available, I still go back to my ancient French mouli – a hand-worked purée maker. You can still buy them in most kitchen shops and they are dishwasher-safe.

Smoked salmon with lentils, onions and carrots

Our local fishmonger is fantastic and the shop is always full of customers. People come from far and wide, and queue patiently halfway down the street to collect their orders of oysters, crab, lobster, prawns, langoustines, tiny brown shrimps, scallops and giant whelks. Everything is beautifully displayed on beds of ice. His wife gave me this recipe and it works just as well with all the smoked fish except haddock.

BENEFITS

■ This dish is one of the best for omega-3 fatty acids.

■ It also has vitamin D, which you must have to absorb calcium.

■ It contains a whole day's fibre and folic acid, as well as large quantities of iron, zinc, copper, potassium and manganese.

■ In addition, it has more than enough protein for a superactive day.

Serves 4

25g (1oz) unsalted butter

2 tbsp rapeseed oil

1 large red onion, chopped

1 large carrot, peeled and cubed

250g (9oz) green Puy lentils, well washed and drained

400ml (14fl oz) vegetable stock

1 bouquet garni

coarse sea salt and freshly ground black pepper

1 tbsp balsamic vinegar

125ml (4fl oz) low-fat natural yogurt

4 slices of smoked salmon, organic if possible

small bunch chives

Melt the butter and oil in a thick-bottomed saucepan over a low heat. Sweat the onion and carrot in the pan until soft but not brown – about 10 minutes. Add the lentils, stir well to coat and cook for another 10 minutes. Pour in just enough stock to cover them and simmer for 20 minutes. Add the bouquet garni, a pinch of salt and plenty of pepper, and simmer for a further 15 minutes or until the lentils are just cooked. Strain and leave to cool, covered.

Whisk the vinegar and yogurt in a bowl and lightly season. To serve, arrange the lentils on an oval platter, pour on the yogurt dressing, place the rolled slices of salmon on top and decorate with the chives.

chapter 5
salads and leaves

lettuce • chard • spinach

Lettuce

These days there are so many varieties of lettuce available, it's possible to harvest one or another for almost 12 months of the year. Unless you live in the freezing wastelands, you won't even need a heated greenhouse, just a conservatory, some cloches, a miniature plastic tunnel or a roll of garden fleece.

Considering that lettuce is 95 per cent water, and an average portion contains just 7 calories, you may be forgiven for thinking it not worth eating. Unless you choose the right varieties, you could be correct in terms of nutritional value, although all lettuces can be used to embellish tasty salads that include other high-nutrient ingredients. In principle, the darker the colour the more nutritious the leaf, so shredded iceberg is the poorest relative. Dark green cos, or romaine, is good, but red-leaved varieties are by far the best, lollo rosso for example.

Hardy varieties, such as corn salad (also known as lamb's lettuce or mache), are the most welcome of winter salads. They are perfect as cut-and-come-again crops and will survive outside with just a little protection through the hardest of winters.

READY FOR BED

All modern lettuces are descended from the wild lettuce, a favourite of the ancient Romans. As well as eating them, they used the milky juice from the broken stems to induce sleep. Today's lettuces contain the same distant relative of morphine in the juice and, although less potent, a bedtime lettuce sandwich will help you sleep.

Lettuces are usually sown in an open position to make the most of the sunshine, but as it gets warmer, sow them in light shade, because those grown in hot spots are liable to produce bitter leaves.

Keep lettuces well watered, because they are prone to bolting if stressed.

Cultivation

Lettuce can be grown in a wide range of soils, but loose, fertile, sandy loam soils, well supplied with organic matter, are best. The soil should be well drained and moist but not soggy. Lettuce does not have an extensive root system, so ensure there is an adequate supply of moisture and nutrients for proper development.

Lettuce seeds are very small, so a well-prepared seedbed is essential. Large clods of soil will not allow proper seed-to-soil contact. If sowing outside, rake the surface to a fine, crumbly texture. Mark out the row with a garden line and make a drill by creating a long, shallow groove in the soil approximately 1cm (½in) deep. When the seedlings emerge, thin them out to leave 10cm (4in) gaps between the plants.

If you are starting off your lettuces in a greenhouse, sow in trays from late winter to early spring, so the seedlings are ready for planting outside as soon as the frosts pass. Wait until they are 5 to 8cm (2 to 3in) high, dig a series of small holes and drop one in each. Space them approximately 15cm (6in) apart for narrow varieties, or 30cm (12in) apart for those with larger heads.

An organic mulch will help suppress weeds and keep soil temperatures cool. Pull weeds by hand, taking care not to damage the roots of the plants.

WHY EAT LETTUCE?

VITAMIN K Darker green and red-leaved lettuces contain an enormous amount of this vitamin.
VITAMINS A AND C They are also an excellent source of vitamin A and a good source of vitamin C.
FOLIC ACID Their high content of folic acid makes them a good choice for women of child-bearing age.
MINERALS They are a good source of minerals, especially manganese.
B VITAMINS Useful quantities.
FIBRE Useful quantities.

HARVESTING AND STORING

Your lettuces are ready when they are full-size but still young and tender – over-mature lettuce can taste bitter and woody. Keep salad leaves in a sealed bag in the fridge for two or three days; long-term storage of fresh lettuce is impossible. If you're using whole plants rather than cut leaves, storing with the root intact will prevent wilting. This is especially true with corn salad.

HOW TO COOK

Generally speaking, it's best to eat lettuces raw and very fresh. However, as a gardener you'll get gluts, so use them to make a fine soup, which can be frozen, or braise them with peas as a vegetable, like the French do. This dish is delicious cold the next day with ham, chicken, fish or other leftovers.

Making a salad box

Wooden crates or boxes make great containers for growing salad – they're sturdy, the perfect size, can be left out in all weathers and look even more attractive as they age.

As for nearly all containers, start by drilling several evenly spaced drainage holes in the base of the wooden box (the easiest way to do this is to turn the box upside down).

Layer the bottom with bits of broken pots to aid drainage. Cover with a mixture of one-third sharp sand, one-third soil, and one-third peat-free potting compost, all thoroughly mixed. Water the box so the mixture is damp.

Carefully plant your lettuce seedlings. Make sure they are evenly spaced, and use a thick pencil to make a hole in the soil. Try to avoid damaging the delicate roots when removing the young plants from their pots.

Water the box regularly (either early in the morning or late in the evening) and keep a watchful eye for slugs or snails. Within a couple of weeks you'll be able to pick leaves as and when you need them.

Chard

This vegetable is one of the most remarkably nutritious of all the leaf plants. Eating chard combines the same protective benefits as you'd get from kale, broccoli, beetroot and even strawberries: the leaves contain many different antioxidants, heart-protective substances and anti-cancer chemicals.

Often referred to as Swiss chard, although it doesn't come from Switzerland, chard is also called silver beet and seakale beet, among many other names. Chard, like beetroot to which it's related, evolved from sea beet, and originates from Mediterranean regions. It was well-known in ancient times – mentioned by Aristotle – when it was much appreciated for its medicinal properties. Chard is cruciferous, that is it protects against cancer, and is full of vitamins and minerals – and it has no fat, no cholesterol and only a tiny amount of salt.

The coloured varieties – the stems may be bright pink, red, orange or white – contain a range of highly protective carotenoids, and all vegetables in this family produce slow-release energy, which means they help control blood-sugar levels and prevent wild fluctuations.

This is a fantastic all-year-round, health-giving plant, which can be harvested from one summer to the next. It's best to cut leaves frequently to avoid bolting – and make sure you remove flowering heads as soon as they appear.

Cultivation

Chard does best in an open, sunny position, and in fertile, moist soil. For a spring crop, sow late the previous summer

Using a sharp gardening knife to cut through the base of leaf stems is much better than scissors or breaking them off. This is double value for your work, as you have two vegetables in one. Use the leaves like spinach (see right) and the stalks steamed and served with a little butter and black pepper.

and bear in mind that the plants may need protection if the winter is very severe.

For a summer crop, which you can usually harvest well into the autumn, sow the seeds in a seed tray and plant out the seedlings in late spring, when they're big enough to handle. If you plan to use the young leaves in salads, the plants can be about 10cm (4in) apart, but space them out a bit more, about 30cm (12in), if you are going to let them grow to full size. For cut-and-come-again plants, sow seeds directly into the ground in drills approximately 1cm (½in) apart. Rows should be 45cm (18in) apart.

Keep weeds down by hoeing or weeding by hand regularly. It's best to keep the soil moist during dry spells, although plants can withstand a drought well.

WARNING!

Chard contains quite a lot of oxalic acid, which can crystallize and form kidney and gallstones. For this reason, anyone with kidney or gall bladder problems should avoid it.

WHY EAT CHARD?

VITAMINS K, A, C AND E Chard contains vast amounts of vitamin K, is rich in vitamin A, high in vitamin C and has useful amounts of vitamin E.
MINERALS Valuable amounts of magnesium and iron.
FIBRE A good source.

HARVESTING AND STORING

The leaves wilt quickly after cutting, so use them as soon as possible. You can wash, blanch and freeze the leaves, but, in my experience, frozen stems just go mushy.

HOW TO COOK

Don't eat the leaves raw. Boil in a minimal amount of water, or steam, and discard the water, which will contain acids from the plant. Once cooked, squeeze out surplus water and eat as a salad with dressing or serve as a cooked vegetable.

Use the cut-up stems as a separate vegetable, boiled or sautéed. This may sound a little strange, but the cooked stems are delicious served as 'soldiers' with boiled or poached eggs. They also taste delicious covered with béchamel sauce.

Spinach

Unfortunately, the cartoon character Popeye was wrong. Although spinach contains a good supply of iron, it also has oxalic acid, which prevents the iron from being absorbed. In spite of that, spinach leaves are still, weight-for-weight, one of the most nutritious of all plants, so Popeye got plenty of other good things.

Spinach probably comes from the Middle East, and arrived in England and France in the fourteenth century via Nepal, ancient China and then Spain. It was, apparently, a favourite of Catherine de' Medici, who was born in Florence, and many recipes based on spinach are still referred to as 'Florentine'.

The enormous amount of vitamin K contained in spinach, combined with the calcium and magnesium, is a serious protector of your bones, making spinach one of the most important vegetables for all of us – but especially for women, who have a higher risk of osteoporosis (brittle bone disease) in later life.

As well as huge quantities of vitamins and minerals, spinach provides phytonutrients that reduce the risk of stomach, breast and prostate cancers, help prevent heart disease and are some of the most powerful of all the natural anti-inflammatory chemicals. Regular consumption of spinach also means you're much less likely to develop age-related macular degeneration (AMD), the most common cause of blindness in older people.

There are two types of spinach – winter (perpetual) and summer (true). Winter spinach is a cut-and-come-again crop, the leaves are generally darker and it has a stronger flavour than summer spinach.

Birds love spinach. If this is a problem, cover your plants with a net.

Summer spinach lasts a limited amount of time; once the plant is cut it will die off, and it often bolts and goes to seed more quickly than the winter type.

Cultivation

Spinach will grow in almost any soil, but it prefers to be mixed with well-rotted manure or compost. Try planting it between some tall vegetables that offer a little light shade, because it will bolt if the soil is allowed to dry out.

Sow winter spinach from late summer to early autumn, and summer spinach in the spring. If you're starting summer spinach inside, plant it out as soon as the soil has warmed up and the risk of frost has passed. Plant both in drills 2.5cm (1in) deep and water in well.

Winter spinach seeds should be sown at intervals of 23cm (9in), and summer spinach seedlings thinned to a distance of 8cm (3in). Rows should be about 30cm (12in) apart for summer spinach; 45cm (18in) for winter spinach.

Repeat sowings of summer spinach every two to three weeks to provide you with a continuous crop throughout the season.

Keep weeds down by gently hoeing or weeding by hand, and be sure to water well, particularly in dry spells.

WHY EAT SPINACH?

VITAMINS Spinach contains huge amounts of vitamins K and A, and is a valuable source of vitamins C, B2 and E.
MINERALS It is full of manganese and folic acid and high in magnesium and iron. It also contains good amounts of calcium and potassium.
PHYTONUTRIENTS Spinach contains some of the most important of these vital chemicals.

HARVESTING AND STORING

Pull up summer spinach as soon as it's ready. When you cut winter spinach, leave a short stump to grow again. If you plant some of the small-leaf varieties, you should have an excellent cut-and-come-again harvest for all but the hottest months of the year.

You can't store spinach except if you freeze it.

HOW TO COOK

Small, young spinach leaves are delicious eaten raw in salads. Mature leaves can be quickly wilted with a little butter in a pan, and served topped with a poached egg and a fresh tomato. Add a thick slice of wholemeal bread for a complete and nourishing meal.

One of my favourite dishes uses washed wet spinach leaves cooked in a large saucepan, with no extra water, until just soft, then eaten warm, sprinkled with chopped raw onion, a squeeze of lemon juice, a dash of olive oil and a little nutmeg – just like the Italians do.

Sweet and sour sorrel and rocket salad

Sorrel and rocket were both great favourites of the Romans and have been used throughout Europe since the days of the Caesars, but sadly they vanished from the English kitchen not long after the reign of Henry VIII. Rocket has made a comeback in the last 20 years or so, but sorrel has yet to return to popular status in the UK.

If you have fresh young dandelions in a dog-free garden, do use the inner, bright green leaves in this and other salads. You can buy them in French street markets where they are called *pis en lit* (wet-the-bed).

Serves 4 as a side salad

3 thick slices wholemeal bread

2 tbsp olive oil

1 level tsp paprika – more if you like spicier food

1 tsp coarse sea salt

2 tsp raspberry vinegar

2 pinches golden caster sugar

3 tbsp extra virgin olive oil

2 large handfuls sorrel leaves, washed, thick stalks removed

2 large handfuls rocket, washed, thick stalks removed

1 large handful dandelion leaves, (optional)

2 little gem lettuces, washed and coarsely torn

Use a small biscuit cutter to make about 12 rounds from the bread. Put the olive oil in a frying pan, heat to medium, add the bread and cook gently for about 5 minutes each side until golden. Remove and drain on kitchen paper.

In a bowl, thoroughly mix the paprika and salt. Toss in the croûtons and set aside.

Mix together the raspberry vinegar, sugar, extra virgin olive oil and 2 tablespoons of water, whisking well until it emulsifies.

Put the salad leaves in a large salad bowl. Arrange the paprika croûtons on top and spoon over the dressing just before serving.

TIP: Sorrel contains oxalic acid, which, in excess, can exacerbate joint problems and is not great for your health if you consume very large amounts several times a week.

BENEFITS

- Rocket is low in calories (only 5 in 20g) and has vitamins A, C and K. Do not confuse with American 'rocket salad'–another name for winter cress.
- Sorrel is rich in vitamin C, fibre and some blood-cleansing chemicals.
- Dandelion leaves are an effective diuretic and help with painful and swollen hands, feet, ankles and breasts. They are one of the earliest available sources of vitamin C and iron after the winter.

Scallops with chard and hazelnuts

I have to admit that I don't particularly like seafood. My wife and many of my friends love it, however, and I'm very happy to use it in recipes. Chard, on the other hand, is one of my favourite foods. Together with the toasted hazelnuts, it adds a wonderful flavour to this dish.

BENEFITS

- Scallops contain omega-3 fatty acids.
- Chard is full of vitamins and minerals, protects against cancer and is particularly good for maintaining healthy bones.
- Hazelnuts are very low in salt and rich in vitamin E and magnesium, making this a great healthy heart recipe.

Serves 2

2 tbsp whole hazelnuts

60g (2oz) unsalted butter

8 queen scallops

3 tbsp fresh thyme leaves

3 shallots, very finely chopped

8 large chard leaves, preferably one of the red-stemmed varieties

1 tbsp balsamic vinegar

ground white pepper

First toast the hazelnuts in a dry frying pan until just brown and crunchy. Set aside to cool and then chop them coarsely.

Gently heat the butter in a large frying pan until it's golden – about 3 minutes – then pour it into a small dish and set aside.

Season the scallops with pepper and half the thyme and cook in the frying pan for about 2 minutes each side, until opaque. Remove the scallops from the pan and keep them warm in the oven.

Put the shallots, the rest of the thyme and the toasted hazelnuts into the pan and stir on a medium heat for 1 minute.

At the same time, plunge the chard leaves into boiling water for 30 seconds. Then place in a colander and rinse with cold water to stop them cooking any more. Rest the colander on a saucepan with 1cm (½in) of boiling water in the bottom and steam gently to keep the chard leaves hot.

Take the frying pan off the heat, add the reserved butter and balsamic vinegar. Arrange the chard between two dishes and top with the scallops, then the shallots, thyme and hazelnuts.

Eat at once, accompanied with a crisp, dry white wine, such as Chablis.

Lamb's lettuce, raspberry and asparagus salad

Adding fruit to a salad is a brilliant idea – you get a whole range of nutrients from this recipe, it looks gorgeous and the sweet dressing is delightfully different. You could use spinach instead of – or as well as – lamb's lettuce.

BENEFITS

■ Lamb's lettuce and spinach are full of vitamin C, folic acid and betacarotene.

■ Raspberries are high in antioxidants.

■ Kidney-protective phytochemicals come from the asparagus.

Serves 2

3 tbsp extra virgin olive oil

1 tbsp white wine vinegar

2 tbsp runny honey

6 spears young asparagus, woody ends removed

2 large handfuls lamb's lettuce and/or baby spinach

110g (4oz) fresh raspberries

2 large sprigs redcurrants

Make the dressing by mixing together the olive oil, vinegar and honey and whisking until they are well combined. Put in the fridge until needed.

Simmer the asparagus in hot water until just tender – about 4 minutes. Plunge into cold water and drain.

Pile the lamb's lettuce and/or spinach into two bowls. Mix in the asparagus, top with the raspberries and redcurrants and sprinkle over the dressing.

Lettuce braised with peas

This is one of my favourite recipes for garden-fresh food when there is a surplus of produce. Here we have a classic of French cooking, but a dish that is a stranger to most British or American domestic kitchens, despite being quick and easy to prepare. Serve it with chicken, lamb or other meat dishes, or omit the bacon and use it with vegetarian bean recipes.

BENEFITS

- The additional vitamin C in this dish, more than a day's dose, helps the absorption of iron in the peas.
- The recipe also contains a good supply of B vitamins, other minerals and fibre.

Serves 4

50g (2oz) unsalted butter

45g (1½oz) lean back bacon, chopped

1 medium onion, very finely chopped

450g (1lb) peas, fresh or frozen

300ml (10fl oz) vegetable stock

1 medium green lettuce, washed and shredded

1 small oak leaf lettuce, washed and shredded

1 handful mint, stripped from any coarse stems and finely shredded

Heat a frying pan over a moderate heat and add the butter and bacon. Fry for two minutes. Add the onion and fry for 4–5 minutes until the onion is soft but not brown.

Stir in the peas and pour in the stock. Bring to a simmer before adding the shredded lettuce. Stir well and cover with a tight-fitting lid. Simmer for 2–3 minutes, sprinkle in the mint and serve straightaway.

Lettuce soup with bacon

Lettuces are the easiest thing in the world to grow and if you are inundated with them, try this soup. Actually, this dish is far more than just a bit of garden-glut cooking. Even if you plant little and often so that you spread the harvesting period, it's worth using some of your lettuces in this excellent, health-promoting recipe.

Serves 4

1 medium onion, chopped

½ clove garlic, chopped

150g (5oz) lean bacon – smoked if you like – cut into smallish strips

2 tbsp olive oil

1.2 litres (2 pints) chicken stock

2 large red lettuces, thoroughly washed and shredded

225ml (8fl oz) bio yogurt

1 handful fennel leaves, snipped

Soften the onion, garlic and bacon in the oil. Add the stock and bring to the boil. Stir in the lettuce and simmer gently for 10 minutes. Add the yogurt and serve hot or cold, sprinkled with the snipped fennel leaves.

BENEFITS

- This soup contains valuable quantities of fibre, calcium, magnesium and selenium, and more than a daily dose of vitamins A and K.
- Using home-made chicken stock adds all the enzymes that turn a bowl of this soup into nature's own bug fighter for coughs, colds and viral infections.
- The yogurt provides calcium.
- Fennel aids digestion.

Plaice parcels

I just adore fish – and plaice is one of my all-time favourites. Wrapping these fillets in a neat parcel of fresh chard leaves may seem fiddly, but believe me, it isn't, and the accompanying tomato and garlic sauce is extremely easy to make. The delicate flavour and the excellent health benefits are worth any effort involved in preparing this recipe.

BENEFITS

- Fat-free protein and minerals from the fish.
- Chard provides vitamin C and beta-carotene.
- Tomatoes contain cancer-preventive lycopene.
- Shallots and garlic are rich in heart-protective phytochemicals.

Serves 4

4 large chard leaves

4 plaice fillets, skinned

350ml (12fl oz) vegetable or fish stock

1 clove garlic, finely chopped

2 shallots, finely chopped

2 tbsp olive oil

200g (7 oz) chopped tomatoes

1 tbsp flat-leaf parsley, chopped

Preheat the oven to 180°C/350°F/gas 4.

Blanch the chard in a pan of hot water for 3 minutes. Strain, refresh in cold water, then dry. Put the fish fillets on a chopping board and halve them lengthwise. Lay each fillet on a chard leaf and roll up reasonably tightly. Put the fillets into an ovenproof dish into which they fit snugly. Pour over the stock. Cover and bake in the oven for 20 minutes.

Meanwhile, sauté the garlic and shallots in the oil, stir in the tomatoes and parsley and heat. Serve the fish parcels with the sauce on the side.

Polenta baked with chard and cheese

Typical peasant food from Italy, this sustaining dish is wonderful as a light lunch or supper – and great to prepare early for when the kids come home from school. The combination of polenta, chard and cheese makes an extremely well-balanced meal. If there is anything left over, enjoy it cold the following day.

BENEFITS

- Polenta is a good source of folic acid, fibre and B vitamins.
- The cheese has protein and calcium.
- Chard provides vitamins A, C and K, and iron.

Serves 4

1 tbsp olive oil

2 cloves garlic, finely chopped

275g (10oz) young chard leaves, finely chopped

450g (1lb) instant polenta

75g (3oz) mixed grated Parmesan and Gruyère cheese

Preheat the oven to 200°C/400°F/gas 6.

Heat the oil in a large frying pan and sauté the garlic gently until soft but not browned. Add the chard and stir until wilted. Set aside.

Cook the polenta according to the packet instructions, then spoon half into a lightly oiled, ovenproof dish. Spread the chard mixture over the top, cover with the rest of the polenta and sprinkle with the cheese. Bake for about 15 minutes, until the cheese is bubbling and golden.

Asian chard toasts

These very simple Indian delights have the wonderful combination of sweetness from the sultanas, freshness from the chard and spiciness from the garam masala. You can serve them as nibbles on diagonal, toasted slices of French bread, but I think they make such a great starter or light meal, why waste the effort on pre-dinner snacks? Also the naan bread has very little fat or salt. Using 'rainbow' chard adds not only visual appeal but also lots of extra nutrients.

BENEFITS

- Chard is one of the most nutrient-rich of all vegetables. The coloured stalks boost the beta-carotene content to exceptional levels.
- One portion of these chard toasts provides several days worth of vitamins K, A and C, as well as magnesium, manganese, potassium and even some iron from the sultanas.
- The natural sugars in the sultanas provide energy.
- Naan bread has good carbohydrates.

Serves 2

15g (1 tbsp) sultanas

1 clove garlic, finely minced

15ml (1 tbsp) olive oil

275g (10oz) young chard with stalks, finely chopped

15g (1 tbsp) pine nuts

45g (3 tbsp) crushed tomatoes

15g (1 tbsp) parsley, freshly chopped

1½ tsp garam masala

2 pieces of naan bread

Cover the sultanas with freshly boiled water and set aside to stand for 10 minutes.

Mix together the garlic and oil and sauté gently until the garlic is softened. Add the chard and cook gently until wilted.

Tip in the sultanas, pine nuts, tomatoes, parsley and garam masala and heat through.

Put the naan bread into a warm oven – about 180°C/375°F/gas 4 – for about 5 minutes. Top the bread with the chard mixture to serve.

chapter 6
summer fruiting veg

tomatoes • asparagus • globe artichokes • sweetcorn • chillies • sweet peppers • rhubarb

Tomatoes

The great joy of growing your own tomatoes is having the choice of so many varieties, from the enormous beefsteak to the Italian plum and the tiny cherry. The availability of colours is pretty surprising, too, including the yellow-and-brown striped Tiger and, one of my favourites, the Black Russian. But whichever ones you choose, there is nothing like the smell and taste of freshly picked tomatoes.

Tomatoes are a staple in many kitchens and quite rightly so, not only for their flavour and versatility but for all the nutrients they supply. In any form you care to eat them, whether raw, cooked or processed, tomatoes are good for you. It's probably best to eat a mixture. They protect the cardiovascular system, are protective against some forms of cancer, and are good for the skin. They're also extremely low in sodium and quite rich in potassium, making them helpful for high blood pressure and fluid retention.

Ripe tomatoes are especially rich in the antioxidant carotenoid lycopene, and this is one nutrient that is more easily absorbed when tomatoes are cooked, so ketchup, purée, juice and sauce all provide more of it than the tomatoes you pick fresh from your garden. Lycopene's vital role in protecting men against prostate cancer has been discovered in recent years – this form of cancer is much less common in Mediterranean countries, where men often eat six or more tomatoes a day.

Ongoing research suggests that eating more tomatoes can protect your pancreas, reduce the risk of heart disease, lower your cholesterol level, protect your colon and even help to reduce the risk of blood clots.

Warning!
As members of the Solanaceae family – the nightshades – tomatoes contain the alkaloid tomatine. This is found in small quantities in ripe tomatoes and is non-toxic, but green tomatoes contain more than double the amount and may trigger migraine in susceptible people. This isn't usually a problem with cooked green tomatoes, but may be with the popular American version of pickled green tomatoes.
  Also, like all the Solanaceae, tomatoes may aggravate the inflammation and pain of rheumatoid arthritis.

Tomatoes can be grown inside or outside, as bushes or vines, in containers, window boxes and hanging baskets, as well as in the ground. Fill up every spare inch with these wonderful summery plants. Outside, they look fantastic decorating a sunny, sheltered wall. Tomatoes grown inside or in a greenhouse will fruit earlier than outdoor plants.

Cultivation

You can either grow tomatoes from seed or buy established plants, which is often easier. If you decide to grow from seed, check the instructions on the seed packet to see whether you're buying an inside or outside variety.

In either case, start the seeds inside by sowing thinly in trays from late winter to early spring. Cover lightly with a layer of seed compost and position in a warm, light place. When the shoots are big enough to handle, transfer them into individual pots and keep the compost moist. For outside varieties, plant out when they are 15 to 23cm (6 to 9in) tall, and place them 45cm (18in) apart. This should be mid-spring to early summer, when all danger of frosts has passed, and is also the time to put in any bought tomato plants.

WHY EAT TOMATOES?

BETACAROTENE AND LYCOPENE Tomatoes are extremely rich in these antioxidants.
VITAMINS C, A, K AND E Rich in these essential vitamins.
MINERALS A good source of potassium and manganese.
FIBRE A useful source
VITAMINS B1, B6 AND FOLIC ACID They contain small amounts of these nutrients.

HARVESTING AND STORING

Pick tomatoes when the fruit is fully and evenly coloured, and don't be disheartened if they don't ripen all together – nature isn't like that. All tomatoes on the vine simply don't ripen at the same time. If any stubbornly remain green, bring them inside and leave them on a sunny windowsill. They will quickly ripen, especially if you leave an apple with them. Make sure you pick all the fruit, including the green ones, before the first frost.

Tomatoes are best stored in a cool place, but not in the refrigerator because they tend to lose their flavour. They should keep for up to five days. Eat fresh tomatoes at room temperature.

HOW TO COOK

Poach them in the same water as eggs for the healthiest of breakfasts. Roast them. Stuff them. Make soups and sauces. Purée to freeze or bottle. Make chutney. Eat them raw in salads. There's no end to their versatility.

Tomatoes need fertile soil and so growbags or large containers filled with fresh potting compost may be your best option. If you're planting in the ground, first enrich the soil with plenty of organic matter and fertilizer, and don't grow in the same place two years running.

Tomatoes shouldn't need much weeding, particularly if they're in a pot or growbag, but remove any yellow lower leaves. It's important to pinch out the side shoots and tops to allow the plant to concentrate on growing the fruit.

Tomatoes like an even moisture level, which prevents their skins from splitting, so don't let the soil dry out. Feed them regularly with a seaweed fertilizer, following the manufacturer's instructions.

Asparagus

Asparagus has been used for medical purposes for at least the last 500 years and it's been cultivated as a vegetable for more than 2,000 years. You'll be amazed at how many new friends you make in the springtime once you start giving out your surplus. I've yet to meet anyone who turns down an offer of fresh asparagus.

There's a strange story about asparagus that says you can tell somebody's financial status by how much of the woody end they break off. The higher up the stem they cut, the richer they are. This just goes to show how much this wonderful vegetable is regarded as an expensive luxury – and nothing could be further from the truth. There's no reason why the smallest suburban garden and the most amateur gardener can't produce one of the truly great foods of the world – British asparagus. All you need is a bit of time, a bit of land, a bit of work and lots of patience in the first year or so. After that, you can look forward to a sumptuous feast of asparagus prepared in every conceivable way. This gorgeous vegetable is good for combating cystitis, fluid retention and constipation, and helps relieve arthritis and rheumatism.

Cultivation

Start with one-year-old plants, or crowns, and you'll get a small crop in two years' time. At this stage, you should cut for four weeks only from mid- to late spring. By the third year, you can cut for seven to eight weeks from mid-spring, when the spears are about 15cm (6in) long. If you start with three-year-old crowns, you may get a bigger harvest sooner, but they are more difficult to establish and you may lose some.

Warning!
Avoid asparagus like the plague if you suffer from gout. It contains a group of chemicals called purines, which can trigger episodes and greatly aggravate the pain if you're already having an attack.

Plant the crowns in early spring, as soon as you get them, and don't forget that asparagus beds are permanent and will keep cropping for 20 years or more.

You need a trench about 30cm (12in) wide and 15–20cm (6–8in) deep. Dig in lots of well-rotted compost or dried seaweed (or fresh if you live near the sea). Cover with a layer of fine soil and make sure you spread out the roots of the crown very carefully before filling in the trench.

In a small garden you can get away with leaving 30cm (12in) between each plant, and a double row of 24 plants will mean that you'll be able to stuff yourself with fresh asparagus. Be very careful of the roots— don't walk between the rows and remove weeds by hand at the very first sign. Liquid seaweed is a great feed.

As the plants grow, they produce ferny foliage. Put a cane at each corner of the bed and run two or three layers of twine right round to stop the wind dislodging the crowns.

The female plants will form berries but don't let these ripen because you'll get self-set asparagus all over the garden, which is troublesome and mostly unproductive. Once the berries start turning yellow, cut down all the fern to 10cm (4in) above ground and use it to mulch the crowns and protect them over winter.

WHY EAT ASPARAGUS?

ASPARAGINE Contains this natural chemical, which is a powerful diuretic. It helps to counteract the fluid retention that comes with the monthly cycle. You'll realize how effective asparagus is as a diuretic within half an hour of eating a portion. Not only will your output of urine increase but it will have a distinctive smell.
INULIN This special fibre isn't digested but provides food for the gut-friendly bacteria that promote natural resistance and digestive health.
FOLIC ACID Asparagus is rich in folic acid, which helps to prevent birth defects and also protects against heart disease.
VITAMINS K, C, A AND B6 Full of vitamin K – 10 spears will give you more than a day's supply. Provides a good dose of vitamins C and A, and a useful amount of vitamin B6.

HARVESTING AND STORING

The season is short – six to seven weeks for mature crowns. Gather the spears early every day, taking any that are more than 15cm (6in) above the ground. Asparagus is best cut with a proper asparagus knife. You should always cut below the surface – getting the knife blade at least 5cm (2in) down. The trick is to cut the spear you want without damaging the mass of new spears waiting to come through. The only good asparagus knife I've found in recent years, other than from a garden antiques dealer, is made by a specialist Dutch tool company, Sneeboer (see page 189).

An ancient Roman proverb says 'Do it as quickly as you would cook asparagus.' How right they were! Pick, wash, cook and eat as soon as you possibly can. Do not even try storing this vegetable for more than a couple of days because the flower top will start to open and dry out, and it then tastes bitter. I wrap the end of the bunch in a damp cotton cloth and keep in the salad drawer of the fridge.

HOW TO COOK

To cook it, ideally use an asparagus steamer, which keeps the tips and a lot of the stem out of the water in a wire basket. This takes about half an hour covered. Otherwise, cook on a wire grid in a saucepan of boiling water without a lid, which takes, at most, 15 minutes.

I think the spears are best eaten simply – hot with melted unsalted butter or cold with a vinaigrette dressing – but you can brush them with butter, grill or roast them and serve sprinkled with Parmesan cheese.

The woody ends of each spear aren't edible, but don't cut them off; simply bend the asparagus until it snaps – if it doesn't, it's past its best – and keep the woody stems and the cooking water to add to soups and stocks.

Globe artichokes

Despite being one of the oldest of cultivated vegetables, globe artichokes, it seems to me, are more popular with eaters than gardeners. As a result, many people miss out on this health-giving member of the thistle family.

The globe artichoke was highly prized in ancient Rome and was one of the most expensive of vegetables to buy. Even in the days of Henry VIII it was more likely to be found in the gardens and kitchens of the wealthy in northern countries – not so throughout southern Europe, however, where this amazing plant was, and still is, valued for its medicinal properties.

Globe artichokes contain cynarine, a unique chemical that is a powerful liver stimulant. Eating them also stimulates the release of bile into the stomach and makes it much easier for the digestive system to deal with all types of fats. The extra bile emulsifies the fat into tiny globules – just like washing-up liquid on greasy dishes – which increases the surface area exposed to digestive juices and speeds up the process. It's no coincidence that the French would traditionally serve artichokes at the start of a fairly rich and fatty meal.

If you have liver or gall bladder problems, eating a couple of globe artichokes a week will help, and they are also good if you have gout, arthritis or rheumatism. With few calories and just about fat free, they are an excellent part of a healthy diet for everyone.

Cultivation

Since growing from seed can be hit and miss, globe artichokes are best grown from cuttings, called offsets or slips. Plant them

Looking good!
Just a couple of plants look great in a flower bed. Grow them against a fence or wall, as long as they get plenty of sun. Green and purple varieties are available and although the purple may look more striking, the green ones are much less prickly.

90cm (3ft) apart and leave a good space between rows, bearing in mind they can reach 90cm (3ft) in height with the same spread. Give them plenty of animal manure and compost, try to keep the weeds at bay with a mulch and don't let the roots dry out, especially in the first few months.

Most artichokes are quite hardy and will survive moderate winters with a covering of their own dead leaves after cutting back at the end of the season. In harsher climates, you can protect them with an 8cm (3in) layer of straw, bark or bracken.

Keep a careful note of which of your plants are the most productive in the first season and the following spring, using a sharp spade, slice off three or four shoots with a good bit of root and plant these to make a new row. The plants tend to deteriorate after about three years, so aim at replacing one third of the bed each year.

You'll never taste anything like the artichoke you cut, cook and eat straightaway. Small artichokes are especially delicious but leave one on each main stem to grow on and you'll have the best of both worlds. When cutting big heads, make sure to take a good length of stem, too, because this keeps the head in good condition for longer. There is a fair chance that the plants will throw some new shoots after harvesting, so with luck there will be a second crop in early autumn.

WHY EAT GLOBE ARTICHOKES?

CYNARINE Contain huge amounts of this bitter-tasting substance, which increases the flow of bile and improves liver function.

FIBRE A medium-sized globe artichoke provides almost half a day's fibre, including inulin – a type of fibre that improves digestion and acts as a prebiotic (food for the billions of good bugs in your gut).

VITAMIN K AND FOLATE A medium-sized globe artichoke also provides roughly a quarter of your daily requirement of these two.

VITAMIN C A reasonable source of this vital vitamin.

MINERALS Contain useful amounts of niacin, magnesium, manganese, potassium and copper.

PROTEIN Globe artichokes contain a small amount of protein.

HARVESTING AND STORING

Globe artichokes do not store well – the leaves harden and open within days of cutting. Once your plants are mature, around the second or third year, use some of the side growth because this will produce larger heads later on. Make sure you cut big heads before they open and flower, and always leave a good hand span of stalk to slow down any moisture loss.

Stand the stalks in a bowl of water if you are not going to use the artichokes the same day. If you have to keep them for longer than a couple of days, put them in a wooden box, cover with damp newspaper and leave in a cool, airy shed or garage, out of direct sunlight.

HOW TO COOK

The very small side shoots with baby artichokes can be lightly sautéed and mixed with pasta. Like the Italians, make sure you cook the leaves together with the peeled chopped stalks to increase your intake of cynarine.

Larger artichokes should be soaked in salt water to remove any insects between the leaves, rinsed and boiled until the base is soft enough to pierce easily with a knife point. Enjoy hot, warm or cold with oil and vinegar, or your favourite salad dressing.

Sweetcorn

Sweetcorn, or corn on the cob, is a perfect vegetable for the Superfood garden because it can never taste as sweet as when you pick it and eat it within minutes. It is reputed to have been cultivated for over 7,000 years but it didn't become popular in the UK until after the Second World War, although it has been a classic dish in the US for a lot longer than that.

Sweetcorn (*saccharata*) differs from Indian corn or maize (indentata) in that most of its carbohydrates come in the form of sugar rather than starch, but as soon as you pick the cobs, the sugars begin changing into starch and gradually they become less sweet. The shorter the time from plant to pot, the more delicious the taste. Low in calories and fat, this is a delicious and healthy food – as long as you don't smother it with loads of butter and salt.

Traditionally, sweetcorn is grown in India, America and Africa, but there are now some very good short-season varieties, perfect for more northerly climates. A lot of corn is grown for animal feed and the production of flour, but the edible sweetcorn, bred specifically for sweetness, can only be eaten cooked.

Don't mix varieties of sweetcorn because they will cross-pollinate and this causes the kernels to turn starchy.

GIVE SUPPORT

Sweetcorn plants can grow up to 2.4 metres (8ft) tall, so if they start to sway in high winds, try earthing them up, which encourages the growth of stabilizing roots. Stake the plants with canes and string if they're looking vulnerable.

Cultivation

Choose a warm spot in full sun, with shelter from the wind and good drainage – but make sure the soil doesn't dry out too quickly.

The seeds are best started off inside from mid- to late spring. Since sweetcorn hates its roots being disturbed, you could try sowing the seeds in a short cardboard tube; cut-down tubes from kitchen rolls or toilet paper are ideal – one seed per tube. Then the tubes containing the seedlings can be planted directly into the ground once the frosts are over, and the cardboard will biodegrade. Each plant produces two cobs.

Plant the seedlings in blocks rather than in rows, to facilitate pollination by the wind. The blocks should be at least four plants deep and wide and the plants 35 to 45cm (14 to 18in) apart. Tap the tassels at the top of each stem when the plants have developed in order to help them pollinate.

Take care not to hoe too close to the plant when weeding, because the roots are near the surface and easily disturbed. Watering is especially important as the young plants are developing and when the kernels are swelling. Watering in between these periods is unnecessary, except in particularly hot weather or warmer climates.

WHY EAT SWEETCORN?

THIAMIN A couple of cobs provide about a third of your daily requirement.
FIBRE AND FOLIC ACID They also give you about a quarter of what you need of both of these.
VITAMIN C A good source.
PANTOTHENIC ACID This is another name for vitamin B5, which is needed to help break down carbohydrates, proteins and fats in the body. Sweetcorn is a good source.
PROTEIN A reasonable source.

HARVESTING AND STORING

Harvesting at the right time is the key to enjoyment. The cobs wiil be ripe somewhere between midsummer and the end of autumn, but that depends on your climate.

The trick is to wait until the cobs look and feel full and firm and the 'silk' turns a darker shade of brown. Open up the husks enough to expose a few grains, which shouldn't be too pale or too dark. Then pinch a grain to squeeze out its liquid. It should be like milk – watery is underripe and thick cream is past its best.

Freshly harvested sweetcorn will keep for a few days in the fridge if you strip off the husks and silk first, but really the cobs don't store well. You can remove all the husks and silk and freeze in bags; or cook, remove the grains and freeze them.

HOW TO COOK

Remove the tough outer husk, peel back the soft inner husk and remove the 'silk'. Replace the inner husk and then boil in lightly salted water. Remove the husks and enjoy whole with black pepper and olive oil rather than the American favourite of melted butter. Otherwise, once boiled, remove the grains and add to salads. They also make very good soup.

Alternatively, you can roast the cobs in front of a fire or on a barbecue. Keep each cob wrapped in its inner husk, or wrap in foil, and cook until the grains are just turning brown and crisp.

Chillies

Chillies belong to the capsicum genus, which, like so many of our favourite plants, are in the Solanaceae family. Conveniently, they divide into hot and sweet varieties, and generally have similar nutritional components. The main benefit of hot chillies is the medicinal effect of specific substances.

These fiery little plants, especially the cayenne, have been used in Indian and South American folk medicine for at least 7,000 years. It was Columbus who brought them back to Europe, where they've been a firm favourite with herbalists since the sixteenth century.

All the other hot peppers, including Jalapeno, Serrano and Poblano, are used for their amazing flavour, but their effects on the body are just as important. They contain a constituent called capsaicin, which is an exceptionally powerful circulatory stimulant. Used fresh, dried or powdered, they help with chilblains, cold hands and feet, the relief of flu and cold symptoms, the improvement of digestion and protection against food poisoning. This substance is now known to be an effective painkiller and is available as a cream.

Cultivation

Both hot and sweet varieties need well-drained, moisture-retentive soil, and if planting in the ground, dig in some well-rotted manure first. They are also ideal candidates for containers or growbags filled with multi-purpose compost.

Start the seeds inside in late winter to early spring. Sow three seeds in each 2.5cm (1in) cell of a seedling tray and plant them

Chillies can be left to dry and used all year round. Try tying them up with string and hanging from a hook in the kitchen – this is known as a rista of chillies.

out in late spring to early summer, when the seedlings are approximately 4cm (1½in) tall. Put each plant in a separate, fairly deep container or, if using growbags, space them about 25cm (10in) apart. Make sure the pots have plenty of good drainage.

Mist the plants regularly to reduce the risk of red spider mite, and water two or three times a week. Take care not to overwater, though, because this will cause the roots to rot. Once the plant is producing fruit, you could help it along by giving it a small amount of organic liquid fertilizer every few weeks.

HOT! HOT! HOT!

Check the seed packets for guidance on the hotness of the fruits, and remember that the longer you leave chillies on the plant, the hotter in flavour they will become, but leaving them beyond their readiness for harvest will result in a decline in further yields.

People with sensitive skins can react badly to contact with hot peppers, so wear gloves when handling them. Otherwise, be careful not to touch your eyes or other sensitive areas, and wash your hands thoroughly afterwards.

WHY EAT CHILLIES?

LYCOPENE AND BETACAROTENE Chillies contain good amounts of these two substances.
CAPSAICIN Chillies are a good source of this alkaloid.
VITAMINS C, A AND K Chillies are a good source of vitamins C and A and contain a useful amount of vitamin K.
FIBRE Small amount.

HARVESTING AND STORING

Pick your hot chillies continuously, starting as soon as they're ready, because this will prolong the fruiting season. Add a few whole chillies to bottles of olive oil and keep in a cool, dark place for a year-long supply. Before any risk of frost, pull plants with their roots and store by hanging in a frost-free shed or garage.

You can use a needle and thread to string picked chillies in a warm place to dry, then store in airtight jars. They will crumble easily for use.

HOW TO COOK

The flavour of chillies is unmistakable, whether they're used in Portuguese piri-piri, Tabasco sauce or your own chilli con carne. I prefer to split the pods and scrape out the seeds before adding whole and removing from the pot when the dish is hot enough for your taste. Otherwise, chop them finely and add at the beginning of cooking.

Sweet peppers

All the many varieties of sweet peppers belong to the capsicum genus in the Solanaceae family. Generally, their nutritional make-up is similar to chillies, to which they are related, but sweet peppers are eaten in much larger quantities, which makes their nutrients more important. They are easy to grow in containers, so you are sure to find space in your garden to cultivate a few plants.

Green, yellow, red and even purple peppers are usually the result of different stages of ripening. They are all so rich in nutrients and so versatile that having your own crop gives you tremendous health advantages.

The skins of sweet peppers, no matter what colour they are, produce natural waxy chemicals, so the fruits are protected against deterioration and nutrient losses. The vitamin C content, for example, remains high for weeks after picking, especially if you keep them in the fridge. The betacarotenes and bioflavonoids mean they help protect against eye, heart and circulatory disease and some forms of cancer; and besides tomatoes, red peppers are one of the few fruits that contain the highly protective chemical lycopene. This makes them a valuable addition to lots of recipes. If you're a smoker, eating a daily portion of sweet peppers will at least give your lungs some protection, thanks to the vitamin A they contain.

Cultivation

Like chillies, sweet peppers need well-drained, moisture-retentive soil. If you intend to grow them in the ground, first

By growing your own sweet peppers, you can avoid the mass-produced, hydroponically grown, tasteless commercial specimens that have a poorer nutritional value.

dig in some well-rotted manure. They will also grow well in containers or growbags filled with multi-purpose compost.

Start the seeds indoors between late winter and early spring. Sow three seeds in each 2.5cm (1in) cell of a seedling tray, planting them out in late spring to early summer, when the seedlings are have reached approximately 4cm (1½in) in height. Put each plant in its own fairly deep container or, if you are using growbags, space them approximately 25cm (10in) apart. The pots need to have good drainage. Water two or three times a week, but be careful not to overwater because this will cause the roots to rot. Once the plant starts producing fruit, feed it with a small amount of organic liquid fertilizer every few weeks. Red spider mite can be a problem, so mist the plants regularly.

WHY EAT SWEET PEPPERS?

LYCOPENE AND BETACAROTENE Sweet peppers contain substantial amounts of these two substances.
VITAMINS C, A AND K Sweet peppers are an excellent source of vitamins C and A and contain a useful amount of vitamin K.
FIBRE Small amount.

HARVESTING AND STORING

Pick your sweet peppers at different stages of ripeness for a rainbow crop and store safely in the fridge for up to two weeks. They freeze well and there's no need to blanch. Left whole, they take up a great deal of space, though, so I deseed mine and prepare in thin rings, lengthways strips or chunky squares, then freeze in bags. However, they have a strong aroma and will contaminate all your other frozen food unless you use at least two plastic freezer bags and seal well. If your bags are flimsy, use a triple layer.

HOW TO COOK

Remove seeds and pith from the sweet peppers, and steam for five minutes. Then stuff with meat or a vegetarian filling and bake. Sliced or chopped, they can be added to casseroles, stews and soups, or used in small slivers in scrambled eggs or omelettes.

The combination of crunch and flavour means sweet peppers are perfect eaten raw in salads.

Rhubarb

This simple, easy-to-grow, trouble-free plant is a healthy addition to most people's diet. Originally from China and Tibet, rhubarb has been used as medicine for thousands of years. The ancient Greek physicians grew it for the roots, which they used to treat constipation. The stalks were first grown as edible vegetables in the Italian gardens of Padua in the seventeenth century.

Although often thought of as a fruit, rhubarb is in fact a vegetable and when naturally matured has a deep ruby-red colour. Like other deeply coloured plants, rhubarb is rich in the antioxidant polyphenols that help prevent the development of cancerous cells. Some exciting new research has found that simply cooking rhubarb in the oven for 20 minutes results in a significant increase in these cancer-protective chemicals.

Unfortunately, rhubarb contains large amounts of oxalic acid in the edible stems, which prevents the absorption of much of the calcium and the small amount of iron that they also contain. The presence of this acid means that anyone with gout or a history of kidney stones should avoid eating rhubarb. The leaves contain even

Remove any flowering shoots that appear because if they are allowed to set seed, this will exhaust the crowns and limit their growth.

larger quantities of oxalic acid and, consequently, are extremely poisonous.

Cultivation

Rhubarb takes up a lot of space, and is a perennial plant. Once established, it will keep producing for several years, so choose your spot carefully – warm and sheltered, but not shady. Once settled, rhubarb doesn't require much attention – perhaps a little liquid fertilizer during the summer months and the usual weeding and watering.

Rhubarb prefers a well-balanced soil that is neither waterlogged nor too dry, but it's not too fussy and survives in most soils. Enrich the ground with plenty of well-rotted manure or compost in the autumn before planting.

Buy 'sets' from your garden centre – these are divided from a mature root, or 'crown', and are much more likely to be successful than growing from seed. Plant the sets from late winter to early spring.

Grow each one separately in a 30cm (12in) deep hole that is wide enough to accommodate the root without squashing. Cover the root with a mixture of soil and well-rotted manure and water in well. Leave about 60cm (24in) between each set.

Take care not to disturb the root when weeding, and water regularly.

FORCED RHUBARB

The pale pink stems of rhubarb you see in supermarkets early in the year have been force-grown in the dark. You can try it yourself by using a rhubarb forcer – a tall covering placed over the plant. Purpose-made rhubarb forcers can be bought or you can use a tall bucket, but don't force the same plant again for two years.

WHY EAT RHUBARB?

POLYPHENOLS Full of these important chemical compounds.
VITAMIN K Excellent source.
VITAMIN C Good source.
MINERALS Contains manganese, calcium and potassium.

HARVESTING AND STORING

If you have forced one of your rhubarb crowns, you'll be pulling delicate stems in the early spring. The rest will crop continually from late spring to early autumn. Make sure you pull, not cut or break the stalks.

CAUTION!
Don't eat the leaves of rhubarb plants because they are poisonous – and don't pull new rhubarb plants until at least 12 to 18 months after planting.

Rhubarb keeps for a week or so in the fridge. To freeze it, either trim, cut and freeze it raw, or cook it first.

HOW TO COOK

Eat rhubarb stewed on its own or mixed with yogurt and muesli. It can be used to make tarts and pies, crumbles, puddings or even tarte Tatin. Rhubarb chutney is a good choice, and combined with ginger, rhubarb makes wonderful jam. Not everyone likes to eat raw rhubarb, but it can be delicious when very young, eaten with honey and cinnamon.

Rhubarb-leaf insecticide

Rhubarb leaves are poisonous since they contain a high level of oxalic acid, but you can turn this to your advantage. Just as they are toxic to humans, so they are to the white- and blackfly that attack your plants. At the first sign of an infestation, put some of this liquid in a sprayer and use on all surfaces of the affected crop, including the underside of the leaves, and repeat as necessary.

When you pull up some rhubarb for the kitchen, cut off all the leaves and put them in a large, watertight container. An old zinc bath tub is ideal.

Fill the container with water to cover the leaves and let them macerate for three weeks. (In the background is a purpose-made rhubarb forcer.)

Strain off the resulting liquid and store it in a closed container until required. Keep out of the reach of children and label clearly as poisonous.

Baby artichokes with pasta

I first had a dish like this when I was working in Rome with Barbara Griggs, co-author of my first *Superfoods* book. My immediate reaction was to say that the only way to eat artichokes was boiled and steeped in butter. How wrong I was! Eating this fabulously healthy and simple dish always reminds me of springtime in Rome and having to ask Barbara what on earth all the farmers' wives were doing selling these strange baby vegetables on every street corner of the city.

BENEFITS

- Globe artichokes stimulate the liver.
- Anchovies provide vitamin D and omega-3 oils.
- Pasta contains good carbohydrates for energy.
- Cheese provides calcium.

Serves 4

15 baby artichokes, no bigger than a Victoria plum, spikes cut off and any tough leaves removed

juice of ½ lemon

½ tsp white wine vinegar

5 rashers lean bacon, cut into fine slices

1 clove garlic, thinly sliced

60ml (4 tbsp) extra virgin olive oil

250g (9oz) flat pasta – pappardelle or linguine

75g (3oz) canned anchovies

2 tbsp freshly grated Parmesan cheese

Halve the artichokes and plunge them straight into a bowl of cold water with the lemon juice to prevent browning. If you are having to use larger artichokes, cut them into quarters and, if necessary, remove the furry chokes.

Add the vinegar to a large pan of boiling water, and then add the artichokes. Simmer for 5 minutes and drain. Sauté the bacon and garlic in half the oil.

Cook the pasta in a large pan of boiling water. When it's nearly done, add the artichokes to the bacon and garlic with the rest of the oil and continue to sauté gently. When the pasta is ready, drain, rinse, tip into a warm serving bowl and mix in the artichokes and bacon. Arrange the anchovies on top and sprinkle with Parmesan.

TIP: When you're cooking artichokes, don't throw away the water. Save it to use as a basis for super healthy vegetable stock.

Four tomato salad

This recipe may sound a bit fiddly, but it looks and tastes fantastic. It's also a huge source of both protective and curative nutrients and is the perfect dish for using all the fabulous varieties of tomato that are seldom available to the ordinary shopper. When you grow your own Superfoods, this is just a sample of the health benefits that are your bonus.

BENEFITS

- Tomatoes provide masses of the anti-cancer chemical lycopene.
- They are also a very good source of heart-friendly potassium and fibre.
- They contain vitamin B6 to help PMS.
- They also contain folic acid for good blood and healthy babies.
- The extra iron they provide helps to prevent anaemia.

Serves 4

4 very large beef tomatoes, thinly sliced (or 2 beef and 2 Black Russian tomatoes if you're lucky enough to find the seed and are able to grow them)

6 good-sized plum tomatoes, quartered lengthways

20 cherry tomatoes, halved horizontally

10 sun-dried tomatoes in oil, drained

1 small red onion, finely chopped

2 tsp fresh oregano

6 fresh basil leaves

60ml (4 tbsp) extra virgin olive oil

2 tbsp hazelnut oil

1 tbsp balsamic vinegar

½ tsp Dijon mustard

Cover the rim of a large platter with the beefsteak tomatoes, alternating them with Black Russians if you've got them. Put the quarters of plum tomatoes in a second circle inside. Fill the centre with cherry tomatoes and lay the sun-dried tomatoes on the plum tomatoes.

Scatter over the red onion. Sprinkle with the oregano. Tear the basil leaves into small pieces and scatter over the plate.

Mix together the oils, vinegar and mustard and drizzle over the salad.

Basque omelette with peppers and tomato sauce

Omelettes must be one of the most versatile foods. They're particularly useful when you have a glut of vegetables or when fresh produce is cheap and plentiful in the street markets. This recipe is a typical example – a favourite lunch dish in the Pyrenees.

The basic sauce uses all those tomatoes that ripen at the same time. It freezes well, and besides tasting wonderful with the omelette, is a great addition to any sort of casserole and is a godsend for those days when you're working late and want something quick to serve over a bowl of spaghetti.

GOOD EGG!

Eggs have had an undeserved bad press for years – I seethe with anger when I see daft people ordering egg-white-only omelettes. They do not give you heart attacks unless you eat stupid amounts, but they do give you seriously important quantities of essential nutrients.

BENEFITS

■ Half of this dish contains a day's worth of selenium and riboflavin, nearly the same of protein, 50 per cent of the vitamins B12 and C and a good dose of phosphorus.
■ The tomato sauce is full of lycopene, good for the heart and protects against cancer.

Serves 2

60ml (4 tbsp) olive oil

1 medium onion, very thinly sliced

½ medium red pepper, deseeded and finely chopped

½ medium green pepper, deseeded and finely chopped

6 eggs

pinch of salt

freshly ground black pepper

Tomato sauce (makes about 500ml/17½fl oz):

1kg (2¼lb) tomatoes

3 tbsp olive oil

1 large onion

2 cloves garlic, finely chopped

60ml (4 tbsp) dry white wine

2 tsp herbes de Provence

1 tsp caster sugar

First make the tomato sauce. Put the tomatoes into boiling water for 30 seconds, drain and plunge into cold water. The skins will then pull off easily. Keep on one side. (If you don't grow tomatoes, or have run out of them, good-quality canned tomatoes will do, but drain off the liquid before using.)

Heat the oil in a large frying pan. Add the onion and garlic and sauté gently until soft but not brown – about 5 minutes. Add the tomatoes, wine and herbes de Provence and simmer gently for 15 minutes, breaking up the tomato flesh. Liquidize with the sugar, return to the pan and heat through, turning up the heat and stirring continuously if the sauce isn't thick enough.

For the omelette, heat the olive oil in a large frying pan. Add the onion and peppers, cover and cook gently for 15 minutes, until soft. Using a slotted spoon, take out the vegetables and reserve in a bowl.

Beat the eggs lightly, adding a pinch of salt and freshly ground black pepper. Pour them into the frying pan and leave on a low heat until the omelette starts to set, and the edges come away from the pan. Add the onion and peppers, then put under the grill until the eggs are cooked.

Slide on to a large plate, cut in half and serve with the home-made tomato sauce.

TIP: You can buy special tomato peelers – like extra fine vegetable peelers – that do the job without the boiling water!

Summer Mediterranean bake

I'm not vegetarian, but I love meals based on vegetables. This is a treat, and many of my vegetarian friends ask for this recipe when they have lunch or dinner with us. Apart from the oil and cheeses, you can harvest everything else from your own Superfood garden. Any leftovers are great eaten cold.

Serves 4

2 medium aubergines, thinly sliced

3 tbsp olive oil

1 medium onion, peeled and finely chopped

2 cloves garlic, finely chopped

250g (9oz) buffalo mozzarella cheese, thinly sliced

4 courgettes, topped and tailed and sliced as thinly as the aubergines

4 beef tomatoes, sliced like the aubergines and courgettes

75g (3oz) freshly grated Parmesan cheese

2 tbsp fresh thyme leaves, stripped from their stalks

Preheat the oven to 180°C/350°F/gas 4.

Sprinkle the aubergine slices with a little salt and bake on a lightly greased baking tray for 5 minutes each side.

Pour 2 tbsp of the oil into a large frying pan and sauté the onion and garlic gently until soft but not brown, then transfer them to a large ovenproof dish.

Sandwich the aubergine, mozzarella, courgette and tomato slices vertically and place on top of the onions and garlic. Squash them down gently until the slices are nearly horizontal. Scatter the Parmesan and thyme leaves on top and bake in the oven for about 40 minutes, until the juices start to run.

All you need to serve with this dish is a large, crisp baguette.

Pesto tomato tartlets

These are so simple and a way to get the youngsters cooking for themselves – under supervision, of course. They look terrific, taste lovely and are highly nutritious. This recipe is for dairy-free tartlets, but if you want to add some grated cheese or a slice or two of mozzarella, that will provide extra calcium and you end up with yummy mini pizzas.

Serves 4

1 sheet ready-made puff pastry

flour for rolling out pastry

2 tbsp olive oil

2 tbsp passata

2 large plum tomatoes

½ jar ready-made pesto

Preheat the oven to 180°C/350°F/gas 4. Roll out the pastry on a floured board and cut into four 15cm (6in) circles (a good idea is to use a cereal bowl and cut around it).

Lightly oil a baking sheet, place the pastry circles on the sheet and, with a sharp knife, cut 6mm (¼in) slashes all around the outside of each dough circle. Cook in the oven for 10 minutes, then remove.

Spread a thin smear of passata over each circle. Quarter the tomatoes lengthways and place two pieces, cut side up, on the pastry. Put a dollop of pesto between each of the tomato halves and a little on each side. Drizzle with a little olive oil.

Return the tartlets to the oven for about another 15 minutes, but check regularly. They are delicious eaten hot or cold.

BENEFITS

- Fibre, vitamin C and masses of lycopene come from the tomatoes and passata.
- The pesto contains the calming herb basil.
- The pastry will give you energy.

Chicken and tomato tortillas

Here is a perfect dish for the Superfood gardener – plenty of produce fresh from your own soil and richer in nutrients than anything you could ever buy in a shop or market. This is the best argument ever against the fools who believe that any attempt at healthy eating means a life of sackcloth and ashes and that the food will be dull, tasteless and boring. Apart from some saturated fat from the cheese – but lots of calcium, too – there is nothing but good nutrition and fabulous flavour in these tortillas.

BENEFITS

- This dish contains enough protein and vitamin C for a day, and masses of betacarotene.
- The garlic and onions provide protection for the heart.
- The tomatoes contain lycopene.
- Sweetcorn provides fibre.
- The spices help to improve blood circulation.

Serves 4

60ml (4 tbsp) rapeseed oil

6 large spring onions, finely chopped

2 cloves garlic, finely chopped

12 fresh green, sweet chillies, deseeded and finely chopped

1 small, hot red chilli, deseeded and finely chopped

6 large tomatoes, peeled, deseeded and chopped

4 chicken breasts, cut into thin strips

2 corns on the cob

juice of 1 lime

1 large bunch coriander leaves, chopped

pinch chilli powder

pinch crushed coriander seed

4 tortillas

275g (10oz) Emmental cheese, grated

Heat the oil in a large, thick-bottomed pan and cook the spring onions and garlic until they are soft but not brown. Add the chillies and tomatoes and continue cooking, stirring, for 5 minutes. Add the chicken, stirring until it is cooked right through.

Meanwhile, using a sharp knife, cut the kernels off the sweetcorn, put them into boiling water and simmer until tender, 5–10 minutes. Stir the sweetcorn into the chicken mixture, and add the lime juice, coriander and spices. Keep warm while cooking the tortillas according to the packet instructions.

Put one tortilla on each plate and spread with the chicken mixture. Sprinkle with the cheese, roll up and serve with a simple green salad and a lime and walnut oil dressing.

Marinated tuna with red pepper and herbs

Raw fish isn't to everybody's taste, but this combination of tuna with red pepper and a delicious selection of herbs and extra virgin olive oil will, I'm convinced, convert the deepest sceptic. So simple and quick, it looks seriously professional.

BENEFITS

- One portion provides half a day's worth of vitamin A and selenium, plus two days' worth of vitamin B12.
- Masses of omega-3 fats.
- A good supply of vitamin B6, phosphorus and protein.
- The red pepper provides a daily dose of vitamin C.

Serves 4

1 red pepper, deseeded and very finely chopped

10 black olives, pitted, thoroughly washed and chopped

1 tsp dried marjoram, or 2 tsp fresh chopped marjoram

2 shallots, finely chopped

juice of 1 lemon

juice of ½ lime

1 tbsp extra virgin olive oil

450g (1lb) fresh tuna, sliced and chopped

dill fronds for garnish

1 lemon for garnish

1 lime for garnish

Mix together thoroughly all the ingredients except the tuna and garnishes. Stir in the tuna carefully and leave in the fridge for at least an hour. Serve on separate plates, garnished with the dill fronds and quarters of lemon and lime.

TIP: Wrap the tuna steaks in clingfilm and put in the freezer for 1 hour. This makes them easier to slice and chop. Don't use a food processor – it turns the fish into purée and loses the wonderful texture.

Asparagus niçoise

The flavours of this dish are just incredible. The piquancy of the capers and anchovy sauce mix so well with the softness of the oregano and the gentle texture of the vegetable. The tendency is to be very conservative with asparagus, but why not break out of the mould and try something that is really different.

Serves 4

110g (4oz) mayonnaise

1 tsp anchovy sauce

1 tsp tomato ketchup

1 tsp fresh oregano, finely chopped – or pinch dried oregano

1 clove garlic, finely chopped

16 asparagus spears

1 tbsp capers, rinsed

Put all the ingredients except the asparagus and capers into a small food processor and whizz until smooth. Shave the woody ends from the asparagus (save for making stock) and simmer the spears in water until just tender – about 7 minutes, depending on size. Arrange the asparagus on four plates. Stir the capers into the sauce and pour over the asparagus.

BENEFITS

- Asparagus is good for arthritis and rheumatism (but avoid if you have gout).
- Capers have a long history of medical use, back to ancient Greece where they were used as an anti-inflammatory food. New research shows that they have powerful anti-cancer properties, too. (A sprinkle is enough to stop the formation of cancer-causing chemicals in grilled meat and so stop the bad effects on DNA.)

Pork and aubergine gratin

This is a good autumn or winter dish, served with a baked potato and steamed, shredded cabbage. Contrary to popular perception, pork can be a healthy, low-fat choice if you buy organic, lean meat. In fact, this recipe is pretty much a nutritional powerhouse.

BENEFITS

■ Pork is a good source of potassium, and a very good source of protein, thiamin, niacin, vitamin B6 and the essential mineral selenium. One portion of this recipe supplies around half your daily needs of these nutrients.

■ The tomatoes, garlic and onions are good for the heart and protect against cancer.

■ The aubergines are a good source of vitamin K, manganese and fibre.

Serves 4

60ml (4 tbsp) peanut oil

2 red onions, finely chopped

4 shallots, finely chopped

4 cloves garlic, finely chopped

5 large tomatoes, peeled, deseeded and roughly chopped

1 bouquet garni

2 bay leaves

4 medium aubergines

900g (2lb) minced loin of pork

30g (1oz) salted butter

60g (2oz) Emmental cheese, grated

Preheat the oven to 200°C/400°F/gas 6.

Heat half the oil in a large pan and cook the onion, shallots and garlic gently until soft but not browned. Add the tomatoes, bouquet garni and bay leaves, and simmer over a gentle heat for 30 minutes, adding a little water if the mixture starts to dry out.

When you are ready to use the aubergines, peel them and cut into 1cm (½in) slices. Don't peel them in advance because they discolour quickly. Fry them gently in batches in the remaining oil and drain on kitchen paper. Add to the tomato mixture and set aside.

Dry-fry the pork in another frying pan, stirring all the time until it is well browned.

Grease a large ovenproof dish with the butter and add a layer of the aubergine and tomato mixture. Follow with a layer of pork and continue until all the mixture is used up, finishing with a layer of aubergine and tomato.

Sprinkle with the cheese and put in the oven for about 30 minutes until the cheese is bubbling. Check regularly and add water if the gratin starts to look dry.

Globe artichokes with two sauces

Globe artichokes are a rather unusual choice to have with dips but they work well. You can make, or buy, any sort of dip you like – salsa and hummus are good, plain mayonnaise is a quick alternative, and a decent vinaigrette makes a refreshing alternative if you want to eat these delicious globes cold. However, the Thai peanut sauce and herb mayonnaise recipes given here make two very different dips to try.

Dunk the succulent fleshy ends of the leaves into the dips, chew off and discard the rest of the leaf. Carry on down through the softer leaves until you get to the middle, remove the hairy choke, and your prize is the succulent heart with more of the delicious dips.

Serves 4

4 globe artichokes

Thai peanut sauce:

50g (2oz) smooth peanut butter

1 tsp golden caster sugar

1 tsp sesame oil

1 tbsp light soy sauce

large pinch ground ginger

Herb mayo sauce:

120g (4¼oz) mayonnaise, preferably home-made

½ handful fresh chives, finely chopped

1 tbsp flat-leaf parsley, finely chopped

1 tbsp tarragon leaves, finely chopped

Pack the artichokes tightly into a large saucepan, completely cover with water, bring to the boil and simmer for about 30 minutes. People say the easiest way to check when an artichoke is cooked is to pull off one of the outside leaves. Much better is to lift each one out with tongs and stick a sharp pointed knife into the base. The artichokes are cooked when the base is soft.

To make both sauces, simply mix all the ingredients together.

BENEFITS

- Globe artichokes help to digest any fat in the rest of the meal.
- The ginger and peanuts in the Thai peanut sauce stimulate appetite.
- Chives, tarragon and parsley also stimulate appetite.

Gratin of globe artichokes

This is one of my favourite springtime dishes, when young artichokes are just starting to appear. It's simple, delicious and tastes just as good cold the next day.

BENEFITS

- The tomatoes provide vitamin C and lots of the anti-cancer chemical lycopene.
- Each portion contains 20 per cent of your daily calcium requirement thanks to the cheese.
- The onions protect your heart.

Serves 4

8 medium (not baby) globe artichokes

juice of ½ lemon

2 medium red onions, finely chopped

90ml (6 tbsp) olive oil

2 tsp herbes de Provence

3 large tomatoes, sliced

110g (4oz) mature Gruyère cheese, freshly grated

Preheat the oven to 180°C/350°F/gas 4.

Peel off any tough outer leaves from the artichokes. Cut off all the spiky tips, quarter and remove the hairy chokes. Sprinkle with the lemon juice and set aside.

In a small pan, soften the onion in half the oil, then transfer to an ovenproof dish and sprinkle with the herbes de Provence. Arrange the tomato slices and artichokes on top and scatter over the cheese. Sprinkle with the rest of the oil and bake for 40 minutes.

Almond and lamb peppers

Stuffed peppers may remind you of student days when you wanted to seem posh. So what? These are delicious and rather more sophisticated variations, still inexpensive and with a lot more nutritional muscle.

BENEFITS

- Full of betacarotene and fibre.
- The peppers provide a day's supply of vitamin C.
- The meat gives you some iron and half your daily protein requirement.

Serves 2

2 tbsp rapeseed oil

1 onion, finely chopped

2 cloves garlic, finely chopped

275g (10oz) lean minced lamb

50g (2oz) flaked almonds

1 tsp cumin

1 tsp paprika

300ml (10fl oz) vegetable stock, preferably home-made

2 tbsp tomato purée

2 medium red peppers, halved lengthways and deseeded

Heat the oil in a deep, non-stick frying pan. Add the onion and garlic and sauté gently until soft but not brown. Add the lamb and continue cooking, stirring continuously, for 5 minutes. Add the almonds (reserving a few for garnish), cumin and paprika and cook for a further 2 minutes, again stirring continuously. Stir in the stock and tomato purée and combine thoroughly. Put the red peppers on top of the mixture. Cover and simmer gently for 15 minutes, until the peppers are just tender.

Put the peppers onto serving plates. Boil the lamb mixture quickly, stirring constantly, until thickened. Spoon into the peppers, sprinkle each with a few of the reserved flaked almonds and serve with boiled potatoes.

TIP: This recipe works just as well with beef or pork, or with leftover cooked, minced turkey, chicken or duck. You can also use rice, lentils, soya mince or a mixture of nuts, raisins, dried apricots and mushrooms instead of the lamb.

Rhubarb open sandwich with strawberries and cream

This simple but interesting dish combines the tartness of rhubarb with the sweet, spicy flavours of the cake. The mix of textures provides an extra eating sensation that will be a new experience for many – and although it may look like self-indulgence, this delicious pudding has good nutritional value.

Serves 4

450g (1lb) rhubarb

2 tbsp dark brown sugar

4 slices good-quality spice cake or gingerbread

450g (1lb) – 1 large punnet – strawberries, hulled

250ml (9fl oz) single cream

ground cinnamon, for dusting

Cut the rhubarb into lengths the same size as the width of the cake and simmer in water with the sugar until soft, but not falling apart. Leave to cool a little. Put a slice of cake on each plate and top with the rhubarb. Arrange the strawberries on the side and pour over the cream. Dust with a little cinnamon.

BENEFITS

- Strawberries increase the elimination of uric acid, an inflammatory chemical that causes joint pain.
- They also contain some iron, which is well absorbed thanks to the high content of vitamin C – just 100g (3½oz) provides twice your daily needs.
- Rhubarb contains vitamin C and fibre.

Rhubarb tarte tatin

Tarte tatin is normally made with apples, of course, but it works equally well with rhubarb. In my view, rhubarb is very underestimated. I love it for breakfast on a bed of muesli, but this recipe really gives it pride of place on any dessert menu. It not only looks good, but it does you good as well.

You can buy tarte tatin tins in specialist kitchen shops, but any deep flan tin will do.

Serves 4

700g (1½lb) very young rhubarb or slightly older stems, sliced lengthways (weighed without leaves)

200g (7oz) butter

200g (7oz) caster sugar

200g (7oz) thick, natural Greek yogurt

1 packet – about 225g (8oz) – ready-made puff pastry

Preheat the oven to 220°C/425°F/gas 7.

Cut the rhubarb into lengths slightly smaller than the radius of a 23cm (9in) tarte tatin tin or deep tart tin. Simmer in 125ml (4fl oz) of water until soft but still holding its shape.

Meanwhile, melt the butter in the tin, adding 110g (4oz) of the caster sugar and cooking gently, stirring continuously, until thick and golden. Arrange half the rhubarb lengths in the tin, like the spokes of a wheel, and pour over the Greek yogurt. Chop the rest of the rhubarb, scatter on top and sprinkle with the rest of the sugar.

Cover the tin with the pastry, trimming the edges but leaving enough to tuck inside the fruit. Prick with a fork all over and put in the oven for about 25 minutes, checking to make sure the pastry doesn't burn.

When it's cooked and cool enough to handle with oven gloves, ease the pastry away from the edges if necessary. Put a plate on top of the dish and flip over quickly so that the tart lands on the plate.

BENEFITS

- Vitamin C and fibre come from the rhubarb.
- The Greek yogurt provides 10 per cent of your daily calcium needs.

chapter 7
squash

courgettes • squashes and pumpkins • cucumber

Courgettes

Both the flowers and fruit of these summer squashes are edible and taste best when they are young and small. Courgettes are, in fact, the young fruits of marrows and originated in Central and South America. They are among the vegetables brought to Europe by Christopher Columbus some 500 years ago.

In America and Italy, courgettes are known as zucchini. Courgettes grow from vines stretching out along the ground, and with their lovely yellow flowers, they can look quite exotic. They take up a lot of space but each plant is quite prolific, so you don't need many of them. Three or four should keep you well stocked for the season, maybe with some spare fruits to hand out to friends. If you leave them to grow on, they become marrows, a peculiarly English vegetable that can be turned into a simple, economic and nourishing meal.

Courgettes may also help to prevent some illnesses. Lots of fibre keeps cancerous chemicals from lengthy contact with the bowel wall. Folic acid, vitamin C and betacarotene protect against colon cancer. The antioxidants that courgettes contain are anti-inflammatory so these vegetables are great food for people with asthma, osteoarthritis and rheumatoid arthritis. The small, but significant amount of copper may also help to reduce the pain of rheumatoid arthritis.

Cultivation

Courgettes need a sunny spot protected from strong winds, with fertile soil that is well drained but moist. Dig in some well-rotted manure or compost before planting.

In cold summers the fruit may not set, due to inadequate pollination. Try picking the male flowers and scrunching them up, then putting them inside the female flowers. The female flowers have little courgettes behind them and the male flowers simply have a stem.

They also do well in growbags placed in full sun.

Sow from mid- to late spring, after the frosts have finished, even if sowing indoors – the seeds won't germinate if it's too cold. Indoors, place a single seed 1cm (½in) deep in a 7.5cm (3in) pot. Outdoors, sow two seeds, 2.5cm (1in) deep and several centimetres (a few inches) apart. Cover with a cloche to speed up germination and thin out as soon as possible.

When the seedlings have produced two or three leaves, transfer them to their final growing position. Discard the weakest plants and cultivate only the strongest of the seedlings, planting them at least 60cm (24in) apart.

Water the seedlings every day until the plants have become established. Never allow the plants to dry out in hot weather and keep the soil moist. Watering is particularly important once the fruits start to form – the more the plants are watered, the more they will thrive. However, if you see a powdery mildew, this means that you are overwatering. Courgettes don't like to be watered on their leaves.

WHY EAT COURGETTES?

VITAMIN A Courgettes are an excellent source of this vitamin, one portion supplying 40 per cent of your daily needs.
OTHER VITAMINS They are a good source of vitamin C and contain useful amounts of some B vitamins.
MINERALS A particularly good source of manganese, as well as containing useful amounts of copper, iron and magnesium.
FIBRE Good source.

To get all these nutrients, eat courgettes with the skins on.

HARVESTING AND STORING

Use a sharp knife and remove the courgettes when they are quite small, approximately 10 to 15cm (4 to 6in) long, unless you are leaving some to grow into marrows. Pick often to ensure a continuous crop and eat as soon as possible. Courgettes can be kept fresh in the fridge for about a week. The flowers should be picked and eaten straightaway.

HOW TO COOK

Courgettes can be steamed, boiled, stir-fried or, in the Italian manner, dipped in batter and fried quickly in very hot oil. They are also a basic ingredient of ratatouille, and about the only squash you can eat raw – delicious washed, dried and grated onto a salad or a bowl of hot pasta. Round courgettes can be stuffed and baked. The flowers are delicious stuffed with goat's cheese and fried.

Marrows halved lengthways and stuffed, or cut in rounds and baked with the skin on, are tender and full of flavour.

Squashes and pumpkins

Squashes are divided into winter and summer varieties, and the winter ones especially, together with pumpkins, are five-star vegetables for your Superfood garden. All of these vegetables make an important contribution to a healthy mixed diet and, as well as that, look fantastic and taste fabulous.

All the squashes are virtually fat- and cholesterol-free and contain hardly any salt, as well as being a valuable source of nutrients. Generally speaking, summer squashes, which include courgettes, pattypans, marrows, selected pumpkins and varieties of spaghetti squash, are harvested younger, have comparatively thin and sometimes edible skins, and they don't store for very long.

Delicious and versatile though they are, squashes and pumpkins don't deliver the same weight of health punch as cabbages, leeks, onions or garlic. There's emerging evidence that they may help protect cells from pre-cancerous changes, but the main reason for eating this family of plants is their contribution to your heart and circulatory health. Eating pumpkins and all the orange-fleshed squashes nourishes your skin and helps with any breathing problems. Whatever you do, don't throw away the seeds. Dried,

Smaller varieties can be grown on a thick support, such as a trellis or an arch, which allows the fruit to hang down. If they become too heavy, they can be supported with nets tied to the structure.

they're a delicious snack and particularly important for men because their high zinc content is good for the prostate gland.

Squashes and pumpkins can take up a lot of room, because the stems will try to stretch out to find space for the flowers and fruits to open out. They also take lots of nutrients from the soil, so they grow particularly well if planted directly into compost heaps or manure piles.

Cultivation

Both pumpkins and squashes need fertile soil, well drained but moist, and plenty of sun. Dig in a significant quantity of well-rotted manure or compost before planting.

If you're starting off from seed indoors, about a month before the last frosts is when to begin. Sow in 7.5cm (3in) pots, 1cm (½in) deep. Transplant outside when the seedlings are large enough to handle and the risk of frosts has passed, hardening off before planting in the ground. If the weather is still cold, cover the plants with a cloche or fleece until the soil warms up.

If you're planting directly outside, dig an individual hole for each plant approximately 30cm (12in) deep and refill the hole with well-rotted manure or compost. Plant three seeds in each hole, 2.5cm (1in) deep and 7.5 to 10cm (3 to 4in) apart. When the

> **TIP**
> For the best chance of growing the biggest pumpkin, leave just one on the plant. While it's still young, put it on a piece of wood or a brick to protect it from pests and keep it off damp soil.

WHY EAT SQUASHES AND PUMPKINS?

VITAMIN A Rich source.
VITAMINS C AND E Good source.
FIBRE Good source.
RIBOFLAVIN Squashes and pumpkins are a good source of riboflavin, which is another name for vitamin B2, needed for the absorption of iron, to aid digestion and to promote healthy skin, hair and nails.
B VITAMINS, MINERALS AND PROTEIN Small amounts.

HARVESTING AND STORING

Winter squashes are best harvested before the first frosts and are ready when the stems start to dry out. They will then need to cure for around 10 days, ideally in full sun outside. If the weather is poor, bring them indoors into a warm, dry place, preferably a greenhouse or cold frame if you have one. Summer squashes are best left on the vine until you need them.

The small buttercup squash, butternut squash, winter spaghetti squash and turban squash will all keep for months in a frost-free, airy shed or garage. Remember to turn the heavier examples from time to time to prevent bruising and rotting.

Since summer squashes are thin-skinned, they don't store well but will be fine for a few weeks.

HOW TO COOK

All the winter squashes make great soup. The flesh of larger pumpkins or the smaller and equally delicious potimarrons can be eaten roasted, steamed, puréed or made into sweet pies or jams. Summer squashes are delicious boiled whole, cut in half and eaten with black pepper and a little butter.

shoots have formed, thin out, leaving just the strongest young plant in each spot. One plant every 46 to 90cm (18 to 36in) is ideal.

Pinch out the growing tips when the plants are 30 to 38cm (12 to 15in) tall to stimulate the side shoots.

Mulch plants well and water every week during dry spells. Water around the plants and not directly onto the leaves. As with all cucurbits, their family name, squashes and pumpkins don't like their leaves splashed with water, which can cause mildew.

Cucumber

The Indians have eaten cucumbers for more than 3,000 years and they were grown by the Egyptians as well as the ancient Greeks and Romans. They're not particularly rich in the major nutrients, but it's no accident that the phrase 'as cool as a cucumber' is part of everyday language.

Did you know that 96 per cent of every cucumber is water? This is what makes them so refreshing and low in calories, just 10 in 100g (3½oz). Cucumbers do, however, contain silica, and the combination of this and their high water content gives cucumber its reputation as an excellent skin food. And they are well known for being good for tired eyes – lying down with a slice of cucumber on each closed eyelid is extremely soothing.

They also have good levels of tryptophan, which helps in the production of some relaxing brain chemicals, so a few slices of cucumber in your bedtime lettuce sandwich will help to give you a good night's sleep.

Cucumbers were first cultivated under glass by Louis XIV's gardener at Versailles. Nowadays, a number of varieties are available, from long and slender, as usually seen in supermarkets, to short and prickly. Cucumbers tend to be divided into the varieties that are better grown in a greenhouse and those that can be grown outdoors. They like a humid environment, so in cooler climates you probably stand a greater chance of success with greenhouse cucumbers, although modern varieties may well tolerate what used to be thought of as less than perfect conditions. Check the seed packet before you buy.

Since a lot of cucumber's nutrients are contained in the skin, it's always best to eat them unpeeled. However, most commercial cucumbers are likely to be waxed with a combination of chemicals that I'd rather avoid. If you grow your own or can buy organic, there's not a problem. Otherwise, scrub cucumbers with a soft brush in warm water before eating.

For cucumbers in pots, tie-in shoots regularly to cane supports, and pinch out the growing tip once the plant reaches the top of its support. Sideways shoots can be pinched out when there are two leaves. Unless outdoor varieties are grown in containers, they don't need supports and can be left to trail along the ground. They need a warm, sunny spot, sheltered from the wind, and well-drained, moist soil.

Cultivation

Sow indoors in spring. Make sure the seed compost is moist and sow a single seed, 1cm (½in) deep, sideways into each small pot. When the plants are big enough, either plant them directly into the ground or transfer them into biggish containers, at least 10 litre (2 gallon) size. Position the containers first, whether outside or in the greenhouse, and push in the cane supports. Allow four to five weeks from sowing to planting. Thin out when necessary, disturbing the root ball as little as possible.

If you're sowing outdoors, leave it until early summer. Then plant three seeds in the ground close together, 2.5cm (1in) deep at intervals of 90cm (36in) for the trailing varieties. Cover with a cloche until germination has taken hold, then thin

WHY EAT CUCUMBERS?

SILICA A good source of this substance, which is great for the skin.
TRYPTOPHAN A good source of this essential amino acid.
VITAMIN K 100g (3½oz) will give you 20 per cent of your daily needs of this vitamin.
VITAMIN C Reasonable source.
MINERALS Small amounts of potassium and manganese.

HARVESTING AND STORING

When your cucumbers are large enough, cut them off the stem with a sharp knife. They are best cut before the heat of the day for maximum crunchiness. Harvest regularly – if you leave old fruit on the plant, new ones won't develop. The more you pick, the more the plant will produce.

HOW TO COOK

Cucumbers are used in making gazpacho, a cold soup, and can be pickled. Otherwise, they are best eaten raw and are delicious mixed with yogurt for the traditional Greek dish, tzatziki, or Indian raita.

out and keep just the strongest plant in each spot.

Whether growing indoors or out, keep the soil moist, but not waterlogged, and feed your cucumbers with tomato fertilizer weekly. Dried-out plants will produce bitter-tasting fruits. Outside in the heat of the day, the leaves will naturally wilt – wet the ground underneath them so that they don't develop powdery mildew.

Marrow, tomato and cheese bake

Marrows are often plentiful and very inexpensive, but despite this, and being quick and easy to prepare, they are a greatly underrated vegetable. Many people turn up their noses at this neglected Superfood, possibly put off by their bland flavour. However, marrows act like a sponge and soak up the tastes of other ingredients. This recipe takes 10 minutes to prepare and 30 minutes to cook in the oven, making it a great after-work family supper dish.

BENEFITS

■ Marrow (with the skin left on) provides betacarotene, vitamin C, lots of potassium, fibre, folic acid and B vitamins.
■ The cheese, tomato and pine nuts add protein, calcium, heart-protective lycopene and vitamin E.

Serves 4

1 medium-sized marrow

400g (14oz) can chopped tomatoes

2 cloves garlic, finely chopped

4 tbsp wholemeal breadcrumbs

225g (8oz) strong cheese (Cheddar or other hard cheese), grated

50g (2oz) Parmesan cheese, grated

50g (2oz) pine nuts

sea salt and freshly ground black pepper

Preheat the oven to 190°C/375°F/gas 5.

Wash the marrow and cut it into 4cm (1½in) thick slices. Remove the pulp and seeds in the middle – I use a large pastry cutter for this job.

Lay the pieces of marrow in an oiled ovenproof dish, large enough for the slices not to overlap. In a bowl, mix the tomatoes and their juice with the garlic and season. In another bowl, stir the breadcrumbs and cheeses together.

Fill each slice of marrow with the tomato mixture, sprinkle on some pine nuts and cover with the cheese and breadcrumb mixture.

Cover the dish with foil, bake for 20 minutes, remove the foil and continue cooking until the topping is brown and the marrow tender – about another 10 minutes.

Serve with a simple green salad for a cheap and nutritious meal.

Courgette gratin

About three months after we moved to France, I was standing in a queue at the street market when an elderly lady in front asked for 6 kilos of courgettes. That's almost a stone! I asked her what she was going to do with so many and she told me she was making lunch for friends, and gave me this recipe. I went straight home and tried it out on Sally and it has been a family favourite ever since. This quick and easy recipe makes an excellent light meal when served with a salad or as a vegetable dish with any main course.

Serves 4

1kg (2¼lb) courgettes, peeled, quartered and chopped

50g (2oz) unsalted butter

sprig of fresh thyme, leaves only

50ml (2fl oz) crème fraîche

200g (7oz) Gruyère cheese, grated

sea salt and freshly ground black pepper

Preheat the oven to 200°C/400°F/gas 6. Sweat the courgettes and butter in a little water. After a few minutes, add the thyme and season. Leave to cook on a low heat until the mixture dries out a bit. Add the crème fraîche and cheese. Transfer to a lightly oiled gratin dish, and bake in the oven for up to 20 minutes, until crisp and brown on top.

BENEFITS

- This dish is a good source of calcium.
- It also has a reasonable amount of folic acid and vitamin C.

No-cook courgette pasta

Pasta is always a healthy option – especially before vigorous and prolonged sport, during pregnancy or as part of a weight-loss plan. The common idea that all pasta is fattening is nonsense – what piles on the flab are the high-fat sauces with loads of cream, bacon, too much cheese and Bolognese made with fatty mince.

This dish is so quick, you'll wonder if it works but, believe me, it does. The heat of the pasta partially cooks the grated courgette. Wholemeal pasta has more fibre and B vitamins, but I find most varieties on the heavy side. If you're eating a healthy diet anyway, there's no need to sacrifice the pleasure of good, ordinary pasta. I always serve this dish with a traditional Italian tomato and onion salad.

Serves 4

1 tsp olive oil

2 pinches salt

450g (1lb) spaghettini

300g (10oz) courgettes, trimmed, washed and unpeeled

10g (½oz) unsalted butter

2 tbsp Parmesan cheese, freshly grated

freshly ground black pepper

Boil a large saucepan of water to which you've added the olive oil and salt. Add the pasta and stir gently to avoid sticking. While it's cooking, finely grate the courgettes.

When the pasta is done, drain and tip into a large, warm serving dish. Add the courgettes, butter and cheese and stir thoroughly. Serve with plenty of freshly ground black pepper.

BENEFITS

- This simple meal will fill you with slow-release energy.
- The courgette skin is bursting with betacarotene, providing you with almost half your daily requirement of vitamin A.
- This recipe also gives you a good dose of fibre and even some iron, calcium and folic acid.
- An accompanying tomato and onion salad provides lycopene and masses of vitamin C.

Duck with honey-glazed pumpkin

It may seem strange to serve pumpkin with honey and sweet spices when cooking a savoury dish, but try it. I first ate this intriguing mixture in a Boer café in Stellenbosch, South Africa, which is in the heart of the wine-growing region. As in most wine-producing areas, taste and flavour are very important, and these Dutch South Africans know a thing or two about good grub. Serve with a watercress, mint and onion salad for lots more cancer protection and a powerful boost for your immune system.

Serves 2

2 plump duck breasts, skin removed and cut into thin strips

2 tbsp rapeseed oil

1 small pumpkin, peeled, deseeded and cut into small cubes

1 tsp ground cinnamon

1 tsp ground cloves

1 tbsp runny honey

Pan-fry the duck strips in the oil, drain on kitchen paper and keep warm.

Put the pumpkin cubes into the pan with the cinnamon and cloves and stir well. Add two tablespoons of water, cover and simmer gently until the pumpkin flesh is tender – about 10 minutes. Drizzle on the honey and stir again.

Arrange the duck strips on two warm plates with the pumpkin on the side.

BENEFITS

■ Skinless duck breasts are a good source of iron and B vitamins and are low in fat.

■ This dish also contains vitamin E, thiamin, niacin, B6, folate, iron, magnesium, fibre, vitamins A and C, riboflavin, potassium, copper and manganese.

Tomato and cucumber salad

This simple, quick salad is a positive cornucopia of nutrients.

BENEFITS

- Cucumber seeds contain vitamin E, and if you don't peel the cucumbers, you will also get plenty of betacarotene and fibre.
- Tomatoes protect against heart disease and cancer.
- Lemon juice has vitamin C.
- Olives contain iron.

Serves 4

4 or 5 cucumbers, cut into 6mm (¼in) cubes – use small, curly outdoor types

500g (1lb 2oz) ripe tomatoes, diced

20 Greek black olives, pitted and sliced

3 tbsp fresh lemon juice

2 tbsp extra virgin olive oil

salt and freshly ground black pepper

1 tbsp fresh mint leaves, chopped

Put the cucumbers and tomatoes into a medium-sized serving bowl and mix well. Add the olives.

For the dressing, whisk together the lemon juice, olive oil, salt and pepper. Add the mint and whisk again. Add the dressing to the salad and toss to coat evenly. Serve with warm pitta bread.

Griddled or barbecued summer squash salad

I first tasted barbecued squash a few years ago in the garden of my oldest friend, *Antiques Road Show* furniture expert John Bly. He put these vegetables on the barbecue one summer evening, drizzled them with olive oil and served them as a starter while he did the macho cooking with fire. It works just as well on a cast-iron, ridged griddle pan. You won't get the smoky flavour, but you will get an attractive scorched pattern on the slices. Any of the summer squashes are suitable – there is a huge variety and they are so easy to grow. Tarragon is the magic ingredient. You really should grow this herb because it is a must in so many recipes, especially French ones, but not always easy to find in shops.

Serves 4

250ml (9fl oz) extra virgin olive oil

125ml (4fl oz) sherry vinegar

large handful tarragon leaves, chopped

2 pinches salt

2 tsp freshly ground black pepper

2 medium courgettes, unpeeled and sliced lengthways into strips about 5mm (¼in) thick

2 orange, green or yellow squashes, peeled and sliced into strips about 5mm (¼in) thick

2 large handfuls rocket

250g (9oz) cherry tomatoes, halved

Put the olive oil, sherry vinegar, tarragon, salt and pepper into a small bowl and whisk well. Brush the courgettes and squashes with some of the tarragon vinaigrette and griddle or barbecue on both sides.

Put the rocket and tomatoes into a large bowl and dress with the rest of the tarragon vinaigrette – they should be lightly coated. Divide the courgette and squash slices between four plates and top with the rocket and tomatoes.

BENEFITS

- This low-fat dish contains betacarotene, lycopene and lots of vitamin C as well as fibre and minerals.
- Tarragon is an excellent appetite stimulant.

Caribbean fish stew

This dish is traditionally made with snapper, but it works just as well with cod. The unusual flavours are a delight, plus you will get an enormous boost of essential nutrients – and it contains no artery-clogging saturated fats or cholesterol.

BENEFITS

- This low-fat dish has an excellent balance between the omega-3 and omega-6 fatty acids, which are so important for heart health.
- Full of protein, it also contains lots of betacarotene, the other important carotenoids and fibre.
- Circulatory stimulation comes from the ginger.

Serves 4

3 tbsp rapeseed oil

1 medium onion, thinly sliced

2.5cm (1in) fresh ginger, finely grated

½ pumpkin or 1 acorn squash, peeled, deseeded and cubed

1 tbsp Tabasco sauce

1 tbsp runny honey

1 tbsp cider vinegar

500g (1lb 2oz) cod fillet, cut into 5cm (2in) wide diagonal strips

handful coriander leaves, roughly torn

Pour the oil into a wok or large frying pan and sauté the onion and ginger until soft. Tip in the pumpkin or squash, plus the Tabasco, honey and vinegar. Add just enough water to cover and mix thoroughly but gently. Place the fish on top, bring to the boil, then cover and simmer for 20 minutes. When the fish is cooked, carefully remove it and set aside.

To serve, put a mound of the pumpkin on each warm plate, lay strips of fish on top and scatter with the coriander leaves.

chapter 8
fruit

currants • raspberries • strawberries • apples • pears
• cherries • plums

Currants

Whether they're red, white or black, currants are nutritionally very important because they all contain large amounts of vitamin C. Surprising as it may sound, these tiny fruits can protect against cancer, heart disease and circulatory problems, as well as all manner of infections. Not only that, they boost the immune system, help to relieve stress and are good for the treatment of diarrhoea.

Blackcurrants, in particular, are an exceptional source of vitamin C – they contain four times as much as an equivalent weight of oranges – and retain it very well. French studies have shown that black-currant syrup loses just 15 per cent of its vitamin C in a year. Most people think the major value of currants lies in their vitamin C content and the fact that this is a powerful antioxidant, but currants also contain substantial amounts of potassium and very little sodium. This means they are helpful in the treatment of water retention and high blood pressure. The least valuable are whitecurrants, which have no vitamin A and don't provide the protective pigments that give the others their colour (white-currants are produced by some cultivated varieties of redcurrants). Redcurrants are extremely hardy, surviving the climates of such diverse geographical locations as Northern Europe, the US and Siberia. They are often found growing wild in hedges and ditches, when the fruit is always red.

Cultivation

All currants are easy to grow and will fit into a small garden. Bare-rooted plants should be planted between late autumn and early spring, but if you buy them in pots, plant them at any time. Blackcurrants like a

The earliest buds appear in late winter, and birds love them. For this reason, it's a good plan to grow your bushes in a fruit cage, but if that's not possible, net them for the winter to preserve the currants. I use old net curtains that I have saved over the years.

sunny site, but the others are subject to leaf burn, so are happier in light shade.

To plant, dig a hole big enough for the roots or pot, leaving a hand's breadth of extra space. Line the bottom with compost, leaf mould or well-rotted manure and a handful of bonemeal. Once the bush is positioned, backfill to the level of original planting – you'll see a mark on the stem – and firm in. Leave at least 1.5m (5ft) between each bush. Prevent weeds with deep mulch, or you can buy a special mat for the purpose. I find these work very well and last for years. Otherwise, it's important to weed regularly, underneath and around the bush. Water during dry weather and manure generously in the spring.

Blackcurrants need to be cut right back after planting, nearly to the ground, leaving just two buds on each stem. Once mature, each winter remove 25 per cent of the grey, two-year-old stems and cut back the older black branches down to the ground.

Red- and whitecurrants do best if you remove the branches right at the bottom of the stem, leaving a 15cm (6in) gap above ground. Allow the bush to grow into an open, cup shape and, like roses, cut off suckers below ground level as soon as they appear. Shorten side branches by half in late spring, then cut right back to four buds in winter.

WHY EAT CURRANTS?

VITAMIN C All the currants are a superb source of this vitamin. As well as its protective value, vitamin C improves the body's absorption of iron.

MINERALS Manganese, potassium and iron are to be found in good quantities in all the currants.

VITAMIN E All currants are a useful source of this vitamin.

VITAMIN A Black- and redcurrants (but not white) are a useful source of this vitamin.

ANTHOCYANOSIDES These anti-inflammatory and antibacterial pigments are found in the skin of black- and redcurrants (not white).

HARVESTING AND STORING

When the currants are ready, snip or pull off whole bunches – you can buy a good harvesting tool that will save you hours of work. Since currants tend to ripen during a short summer period, you'll have a lot at the same time. They don't keep for very long fresh, but they freeze well.

HOW TO COOK

Use currants in compotes, juices, jams and jellies. They're great in fruit pies and make wonderful sorbets and ice creams. They lose little of their vitamin C and none of the minerals or protective pigments during cooking or freezing. Redcurrants are very high in the setting agent pectin. They are good to add to low-pectin fruits like strawberries when making jam.

CURRANT REMEDIES

■ The purple-black skins of blackcurrants are antibacterial and anti-inflammatory. These qualities are put to good use in the country remedy for sore throats: hot blackcurrant juice sipped slowly. An easy way to make this is to simmer half a cup of blackcurrants in 2 cups of hot water for 10 minutes, then strain and add some honey. Alternatively, add boiling water to a teaspoon of blackcurrant jelly.

■ Blackcurrant leaves contain antibacterial tannins and other volatile oils as well as some vitamin C, and you can use them to make tea. Drink it hot to help relieve stress and anxiety, or let it cool down and use it as a gargle for gum infections and mouth ulcers.

■ Redcurrant jelly is antiseptic. If applied to a burn or scald, after irrigating the affected area with plenty of slowly running cold water, it will ease the pain and prevent blistering.

■ Herbalists have traditionally recommended redcurrant juice as a refreshing and temperature-lowering drink for anyone with a fever.

Raspberries

There are summer and autumn varieties of raspberries, the latter being a little sweeter, and although pinkish-red is the most usual colour, you can impress your friends with yellow, orange, purple, black and white varieties as well. Like the traditional bunch of grapes, raspberries should be a gift to every hospital patient because not only are they rich in conventional nutrients but they are also full of exceptionally powerful antioxidants.

Wild raspberries have been around for hundreds, maybe thousands, of years, but they have been cultivated only since the nineteenth century. All the vital nutrients and phytochemicals they contain make raspberries a food to strengthen the immune system and protect against cancer. They are also good for anyone who has recurrent infections, such as candida. They don't adversely affect blood sugar levels and, like all red fruits, the pigments protect the eyes against age-related macular degeneration.

Raspberry plants can be productive for eight to 12 years, and the cropping period during the summer season can last from three to six weeks, much longer for the autumn varieties. They thrive in cool, damp summers, making them the perfect fruit for cooler areas. The canes need support and two posts with three strands of wire strung

The sixteenth-century herbalist Gerard first gave the name 'raspis' to this wonderfully versatile fruit. As well as using them fresh to make pies, ice-cream, jams or jellies, why not make your own raspberry vinegar with fresh fruit, cider vinegar and water? In a month you'll have a wonderful condiment to flavour rich casseroles of duck, goose or other game.

between them does the job well. Use netting to protect the fruits from birds.

Cultivation

Find a sheltered spot for your raspberries and avoid windy sites, since the plants can be damaged by high winds. They are happier in the sun but will tolerate slight shade. The soil should be well drained with no danger of becoming waterlogged.

Bushes are usually bought as bare-rooted plants in the autumn. Make sure the planting hole is big enough for the roots to spread evenly. Once the plant is in position, fill in the hole with a mixture of soil and well-rotted manure or compost, firming it down as you go. Plants should be about 46cm (18in) apart, and if you're planting more than one row, leave about 2 metres (6ft) between them. Water in well.

Let the first canes grow, but cut the first shoots down before they flower. The second-season canes will then fruit. At the end of the season, cut out the old wood and leave the new shoots to grow for next year.

For autumn-fruiting varieties, prune back hard in the early spring, and raspberries will be produced at the tip of the current season's growth.

TIP

Raspberries are notorious for producing side shoots that travel underground and pop up anywhere in the vicinity. Keep an eye out for these shoots and chop them off at root level with a spade.

WHY EAT RASPBERRIES?

MANGANESE Raspberries contain copious amounts of this mineral.
FIBRE Valuable source.
VITAMINS C, K AND E Raspberries are a rich source of vitamin C and a good source of both vitamins K and E.
PHYTOCHEMICALS Antibacterial and antifungal phytochemicals are found in raspberries.

HARVESTING AND STORING

When raspberries are ripe, the whole fruit pulls away from its stalk, leaving behind the hull. Pick them regularly and either use straightaway or freeze.

HOW TO COOK

You can cook raspberries with other stewed berries or add them to fruit tarts, roulades or ice cream, but I think they're wonderful eaten as they are, unwashed and with a little cream or yogurt. You can make lovely jams and purées from fresh raspberries.

Any kind of cooking or processing, especially canning, deprives the raspberries of most of their health-giving pigments. You'll find the highest levels in the fresh or frozen fruit.

RASPBERRY LEAF TEA

For centuries, herbalists, midwives and country women have used raspberry leaf tea as an aid to childbirth. The exact mechanism is not fully understood but the tea appears to strengthen the muscles of the uterus, making contractions more forceful and speeding up the birth process.

Prepare with one teaspoon of chopped raspberry leaves, fresh or dried, added to a cup of boiling water. Cover, stand for five minutes and no more, then strain and drink. Take two cups a day during the last two months of pregnancy. Do not take raspberry leaf tea earlier on in pregnancy, and always check with your health adviser first.

Raspberry leaf tea can also be used as a mouthwash for spongy bleeding gums, mouth ulcers and general soreness.

Strawberries

Among the best-loved soft fruits, strawberries are still regarded as a treat in summer, their wonderfully enticing aroma nearly as good as their taste. Strawberries are very easy to grow either in the vegetable plot or in containers, and they look fabulous trailing down from hanging baskets. The bonus is that they are so good for you.

In medieval times, strawberries were thought to be poisonous – a twelfth-century abbess decided that since they grew so close to the ground, they must be contaminated by snakes and toads. Fortunately, that superstition died out and they have been cultivated to popular acclaim since the eighteenth century.

A myth that has survived, though, is that anyone with arthritis should avoid strawberries because they're so acidic. Nothing could be further from the truth. These wonderful succulent fruits are just about the nicest treatment you could imagine for this painful condition. They work because they stimulate the body's ability to eliminate the uric acid that's extremely irritating to inflamed joints. They are as effective as aspirin or ibuprofen, the non-steroidal drugs that relieve inflammatory pain.

Strawberries are also a very good source of iodine, a nutrient often deficient in the average diet and mostly obtained from fish, shellfish and sea vegetables, such as samphire and seaweed. Eat strawberries for their anti-cancer and heart-protective benefits, and because, in common with all red fruits, they protect the eyes against age-related macular degeneration.

Plants produce the best crop after two years and usually last three to four years,

Anthocyanins are the highly important protective chemicals found in all the red, blue and blue-black berries, fresh and frozen. However, they are virtually undetectable in any manufactured and processed foods, not even in a blueberry muffin. These anthocyanins seem more fragile than most of the other phytonutrients, so if you want the best taste and the best protection, eat them fresh or freeze your own on the day you pick them.

after which they will need replacing. Most varieties produce one crop per year, but perpetual strawberries carry on until the first frosts. The large-fruited varieties produce runners that bear new shoots. Push these into the soil or compost and when they have rooted, separate them from the main plant and there you have some new plants. There are hundreds of varieties, and they have similar nutrient values.

Cultivation

Strawberries prefer a sunny, sheltered site, with good drainage, but will tolerate a little shade. Dig in some well-rotted manure or compost before planting.

Put in your plants during late summer. They should be 30cm (12in) apart and leave 46cm (18in) between rows. Dig a planting hole for each one large enough to spread the roots out evenly, and make sure that the crown is level with the soil. Cover with soil and water well. Keep strawberry beds free from weeds, because these can inhibit the growth of the plants. If planting in containers, plant at any time.

Straw is traditionally used as a mulch, and also serves to rest the fruit and keep it off the moist soil. One story has it that this is how strawberries got their name. Water regularly, but try not to splash the fruit or

WHY EAT STRAWBERRIES?

VITAMIN C Strawberries are full of vitamin C.
MANGANESE Excellent source.
IODINE Excellent source of this trace element.
FIBRE Good source.
FOLIC ACID Reasonable source.
B VITAMINS Reasonable source.
OMEGA-3 FATTY ACIDS Reasonable source.

HARVESTING AND STORING

Pick regularly to encourage new fruit and to stop the birds getting them first. With a careful mix of varieties, you can enjoy this crop from mid-spring to early autumn, depending on climate. They don't freeze or store, so eat as soon as possible after picking. If you try to freeze strawberries, you'll end up with a soggy mash because of their high water content.

HOW TO COOK

You can add sugar and cream, make Romanoff, and turn them into fools, purées and ice creams. You can use them in cakes and tarts or turn them into jam. But I think strawberries are at their best picked, washed and eaten as quickly as possible. I love them chopped and sprinkled on my muesli, and I'm now addicted to my wife's favourite way of serving strawberries – with balsamic vinegar and black pepper. I thought it was bizarre until I tried it.

allow the ground to become waterlogged. Use netting to protect the fruits from birds, and in late autumn and winter, cover the plants with fleece or a cloche to protect them from frosts.

Immediately after harvesting, when all the fruits have been picked, cut off all the leaves to approximately 7.5cm (3in) above the ground.

Strawberry runners

After your strawberry plants have flowered, they will produce long shoots, or runners, which can be potted up to make new fruit-producing plants.

Fill a small pot with potting compost. Place the small, new plant in the pot, but do not detach it from the main plant. Hold the stem in place with a large pebble.

When the new plant has produced its own roots, snip through the runner attaching it to the parent plant and replant in the desired place.

Apples

An apple a day may keep the doctor away, but two will help control cholesterol, protect your heart and circulation and improve your digestion. Even the smell of apples is beneficial because the perfume from a bowl of the ripe fruit has a powerful calming effect and helps lower blood pressure.

Apples have been cultivated for thousands of years and their health benefits are well known. They contain no fat, cholesterol or sodium but are full of dietary fibre. As well as aiding digestion, they help maintain a steady blood sugar level, and if that's not enough, they help reduce the risk of stroke, type 2 diabetes, breast, colon and, especially, lung cancer, and the severity of asthma. Apples are also an excellent food if you have arthritis, rheumatism, gout or colitis. Eating a couple first thing in the morning will even help relieve a hangover, and research in France, Italy and Ireland has shown that two apples a day can lower your cholesterol by as much as 10 per cent.

Cultivation

You don't have to plant your apple tree directly into the ground; you can grow

An ancient proverb says that 'If you can plant only one tree in your garden this should be an apple tree'. Apples are rich in a soluble fibre, pectin, which helps eliminate cholesterol and protects against environmental pollutants. The pectin also combines with toxic heavy metals and removes them from the body.

certain varieties in a container – some have been specifically bred to grow upright with a single stem. You can also train your tree to grow along a wall (espalier), or up a fence (cordon) or in a fan shape with horizontal wires for them to grow along. And don't be put off by the idea that it will take years for the tree to bear fruit – some dwarf varieties crop just two years after planting. Large trees will start cropping in four to six years.

Plant bare-rooted trees in the autumn and container-grown trees at any time of the year (see page 156). Prepare the planting area by digging in plenty of well-rotted manure or compost. The soil mark on the stem should be level with the soil and the roots spread out evenly in the hole. Refill the hole with soil mixed with well-rotted manure or compost. Young trees will need support as soon as they are planted. Water well and keep the area near the trunk free from both weeds and grass, and mulch well.

During the first four years, the purpose of pruning is to train the branches into a framework for providing good cropping for future years. Prune during the winter to provide an open centre and a cup-shaped tree. For a tree that's being trained to grow along a fence or wall, prune in summer to remove stray growth and encourage the tree to grow new branches.

THE BRAT DIET

Bananas, Rice, Apples, Toast – I have prescribed this treatment for diarrhoea for years and it works! Mash the fruit and rice together and eat with dry, wholemeal toast. Alternatively, you could just stick to the apple – grate and leave to go brown before eating. At the opposite end of the scale, apples are a key weapon in the fight against constipation because of their soluble fibre content.

WHY EAT APPLES?

PHYTONUTRIENTS A huge amount and variety of phytonutrients are found in both the flesh and skin.

MALIC AND TARTARIC ACIDS Apples contain both of these acids, which help in the digestion of fatty foods.

VITAMIN C Good source.

FIBRE Wonderful source of dietary fibre.

VITAMIN K Useful source.

HARVESTING AND STORING

Early season apples don't store as well as later ones, but by mixing varieties you can eat your own fruit from late summer to autumn and through to late winter, if you have the space. You can check if an apple is ready by holding the fruit and gently twisting it. The stem should break easily. If it doesn't, leave it for later.

Store on wooden, slatted shelves and make sure the apples aren't touching. Alternatively, wrap unblemished apples individually in tissue or newspaper and store in wooden apple boxes. Keep them in a shed or other well-ventilated place, as cool as possible but frost-free. Eat or cook blemished or damaged fruit straightaway and inspect your apple store regularly. The ethylene gas given off by damaged fruit will cause others to rot too – it takes just one rotten apple to turn the good fruit bad.

HOW TO COOK

Don't peel apples when you cook them because the skin is very rich in nutrients. Whether stewed, puréed or baked, they will lose some vitamin C. The fat-busting potential of apples means they're good with fatty meats, so it's no accident that we eat roast pork and duck with apple sauce, that goose is stuffed with sage and apple or that raw apple is served with cheese.

Apples go well with other vegetables, too – with raw cabbage in coleslaw, for instance, or cooked with red cabbage.

Commercial fruit is often waxed and sprayed, so wash bought apples with warm water and a little vinegar and scrub gently with a soft brush.

Pears

Homer wrote that pears were 'a gift of the gods' and so they are – delicious and full of goodness. They are related to the apple and the quince, and were once eaten only by the aristocracy, but now thousands of varieties are available to be enjoyed by everyone. For the best health benefits, eat them fresh, ripe and raw.

As they ripen, the skins deepen in colour from pale to dark yellow or green to red-brown, depending on variety, and it's in the skin that many of the pear's valuable nutrients are to be found. Pears are often thought of as little more than a sweet dessert fruit, but this isn't strictly true. They have a high soluble fibre content, making them useful for preventing constipation. They help lower cholesterol and eating fresh pears provides an instant antioxidant boost. They're an excellent food during convalescence because they're easily digested, contain no fat or salt and are a good source of fruit sugar, which converts easily into energy. They are also a valuable source of nutrients for people suffering from allergies, because they're the one fruit that hardly ever causes adverse reactions.

Pear trees are native to Europe and many of the popular modern varieties were propagated by Belgian and French gardeners during the 1700s. My favourite, 'Conference', first grew in Berkshire. Comice, Williams, Red Williams and Packham are all popular.

Cultivation

As with apples, planting will depend on the variety. Plant bare-rooted trees in the autumn and container-grown trees at any time of the year. Prepare the planting area by clearing any surrounding weeds and digging in plenty of well-rotted manure or compost. Young trees will need support as soon as they're planted. Water them during dry spells and mulch well.

Pear trees require training during their first four years to create the basic framework needed to produce a good crop in later years. Branches should be cut back severely in order to create an open-centred tree. After that they will need just maintenance pruning – cutting out dead wood. Prune cordons and espaliers as well as dwarf varieties in summer to inhibit shoot growth.

Planting a fruit tree

Planting pear and apple trees will depend on the variety. Plant bare-rooted trees in the autumn and container-grown trees at any time of the year.

Dig a hole at least 23cm (9in) larger than the tree roots. Add plenty of organic material and a handful of bone meal.

Put in the stake just off centre, making sure it is secure. Use treated wood that won't rot and break off underground.

Spread the roots, trim off any damaged ends, place in the hole close to the stake, raising the top of root ball to grass level with extra soil.

Fill the hole, water, firm in, secure with a tie attached to the stake but don't secure too tightly around the tree, leaving room for growth.

WHY EAT PEARS?

FIBRE Pears are an excellent source of dietary fibre.

COPPER They are also a rich source of copper, which counteracts some of the dangerous free radicals that can damage cells and are a normal by-product of your day-to-day metabolism.

IRON AND SELENIUM Pears are a useful source of these minerals.

VITAMINS K AND C Useful source.

HARVESTING AND STORING

Ripe pears are a magnet to wasps, so keep a careful eye on your trees and pick the fruits as soon as they're ready. Some varieties will store wrapped in paper until Christmas – get advice from your local tree nursery – but although it's feasible to store most pears, I've always found it very disappointing.

Pears can be cooked and frozen and they bottle well, although they will lose some vitamin C. Drying is an option, either in the sun or a slow oven or a drying cabinet if you have one. Dried pears are unexpectedly valuable; weight for weight, they provide more fibre, copper, iron and selenium than fresh produce. The downside is that the dried fruit has far more calories.

HOW TO COOK

In salads, pears combine deliciously with nuts and sprouting seeds, celery and watercress. Their sweet flavour is the perfect complement to a sharp goat's cheese, any mature hard cheese and all the blue cheeses. They also work well poached in wine, puréed with yogurt and used as a substitute for apples in a tarte Tatin.

Cherries

The reason why cherries are red is due to the powerful antioxidants they contain. As well as providing the colour, these phytonutrients also bring a variety of health benefits, including anti-inflammatory and anti-ageing properties. The real delight of cherries, though, is that they're still a seasonal fruit, redolent of summer when they're ripe and have the highest nutritional value – and in spring, the blossom is gorgeous.

A huge tree came with my garden and, in June and July, you would not believe how many friends pass by to say hello and just happen to have a bag or bowl with them.

Cherries have no salt, no fat and only 63 calories per 100g (3½oz). Eat lots of them if you have arthritis, rheumatism or gout to help reduce inflammation and levels of uric acid. They also help to lower inflammation linked to heart disease. C-reactive protein (CRP) is a substance found in the blood that is a marker for inflammation in the body. High levels of CRP are associated with an increased risk of heart disease, low levels with low risk. Some specialists now think that CRP is

Of the sour cherries, Morello are wonderful for cooking, bottling and juicing, whilst Acerola is the richest in nutrients, especially bioflavonoids. Cherries contain plenty of potassium and virtually no sodium, so they're excellent for anyone with heart disease or high blood pressure. They're a reasonable source of vitamin C, and also contain significant amounts of bioflavonoids and other plant chemicals, which make them pretty near the top of the list of protective antioxidant foods. It is the ellagic acid content which adds extra value to their anti-cancer properties.

even more important as a risk factor for heart health than LDL (bad) cholesterol. So eating lots of cherries has a strong anti-inflammatory effect, reducing the levels of circulating CRP.

Cultivation

If you do decide to try your hand at a cherry tree, buy one that's less than five years old. Bear in mind that sweet cherry trees are big, growing up to 9 metres (30ft) tall – and there will need to be a compatible tree nearby to facilitate pollination.

Cherries will tolerate either full sun or a shady position. Keep moisture levels steady, because heavy, irregular watering can split the fruits. If planting in dry soil, water while the fruits are developing to prevent them splitting.

Prune the tree in spring and summer. Cut out fruited shoots after harvesting, then in the following spring, thin out young shoots to leave an equivalent number of replacements to bear a new crop.

GO FOR THE BEST

Cherries are a great example of why fresh produce, especially home-grown, is a better source of health-protective antioxidants than a bottle of expensive pills or extracts from the chemist's or health store. A study published in the *Journal of the American Medical Association* has shown that eating fresh produce has a far more powerful effect than taking supplements.

WHY EAT CHERRIES?

ANTHOCYANINS Cherries contain masses of this important antioxidant.
VITAMIN C Good source.
FIBRE Useful source.
MINERALS Cherries are a useful source of potassium and iron.
VITAMINS A, B6 AND E They contain some of these vitamins.
PROTEIN This is present in cherries in small quantities.

HARVESTING AND STORING

The biggest challenge is to get to your ripe cherries before the birds discover them – our feathered friends know all about the health benefits, too! Harvest little and often. Cherries spoil quickly when ripe, so pick daily and eat or cook as soon as you can. The best way to store your cherries is frozen, whole or cooked.

HOW TO COOK

Cherries are versatile and add both taste and colour to your cooking, plus the great nutritional treasures that they supply. Use them in cold soups and juices, or as a smoothie blended with yogurt and other fruits. They are a good addition to salads, and wonderful served with duck or goose. Cherry sauce is excellent with pork, barbecued, roast or pan-fried. You can use them in muffins, pies and tarts, or juiced and frozen in plastic bottles. I bottle mine in very lightly sweetened water, occasionally with added kirsch.

KEEP YOUR CHERRY STONES
Wash your cherry stones well in a sieve, dry thoroughly and put them in a cotton bag. Once heated in the oven or microwave, they make a fantastic hot pillow for the relief of aches and pains in any joint. You can mould the bag around awkward surfaces, such as elbows, knees, shoulders, neck or back, and the stones retain heat for ages. They can be reused many times. So the moral of the story is – always keep your cherry stones.

Plums

Plums were mentioned by Confucius, and brought to Mediterranean regions by Alexander the Great. Now there are over 2,000 varieties, large and small, ranging in colour from green to pale red, dark red, purple and blue/black. They are all members of the Prunus genus, relatives of the peach, nectarine and almond. Prunes are dried plums, and equally delicious.

Plums are among the healthiest of all fruits. They contain no fat, cholesterol or salt, but what they do have are plenty of phenols, nature's damage-limitation tools, which prevent cell damage and the breakdown of the special fats that are so important in the brain. As well as this, anyone with heart or circulatory disease will benefit from eating plums or prunes – and both will help the vision loss caused by age-related macular degeneration.

Fresh, dark-coloured plums, especially, are extremely powerful and protective antioxidant foods, while prunes are one of the richest of all sources of antioxidants – 100g (3½oz) provides more than the optimum daily intake.

Unripe fruits can cause stomach upsets, but the riper the plums become, the more the level of protective antioxidants increases.

The Romans knew around 300 different types of plum and thanks to the Pilgrim Fathers, this important fruit found its way to the New World. Today, the USA is one of the leading plum producers and exports the crop around the world.

Cultivation

If you decide to invest in a plum tree, choose the highest spot in the garden to plant it, and position it where it will get plenty of sun. Some varieties are self-pollinating but others must be near a compatible tree or will bear no fruit.

Plant your plum tree in the autumn or during the winter in moisture-retentive, well-drained soil, and stake young plants for the first five to six years. Hoe to keep down weeds at the base of the tree, taking care not to damage young roots.

Prune a two- or three-year-old tree in early spring. Aim for three to five strong branches at the two-year-old stage, with the branches as horizontal as possible. At the three-year-old stage, eight strong branches should be established with several minor branches spaced around the tree. In the case of an established tree, prune in late spring or early summer. Pruning at this stage should be for maintenance only and to reduce overcrowding.

Keep moisture levels steady, or the fruits may split.

TIP

Most plum trees produce an abundant crop, so be prepared to provide some support for heavy, fruit-filled branches.

WHY EAT PLUMS?

ANTIOXIDANTS Plums and prunes are among the best sources of antioxidants.
PHENOLS They are also full of these important chemical compounds.
VITAMIN C High in vitamin C.
VITAMINS K AND A Excellent source.
FIBRE Good source.
VITAMIN B Useful amounts.
MINERALS They also contain useful amounts of potassium and calcium, and some iron, which is well absorbed thanks to the large amount of vitamin C.

HARVESTING AND STORING

Pick the fruit as soon as it's ripe to discourage wasps and maggots. You can't store fresh plums. They will freeze, halved and stoned, but will then be fit for cooking only.

They freeze well as a purée, but I think they're more delicious bottled, and they make wonderful jam. If you have an abundance of fruit, it's worth trying to make your own prunes – dry plums in the sun, if you live in the right place, in a low oven or in a drying cabinet.

HOW TO COOK

Plums are delicious poached, stewed and used in pies, puddings and tarts. They are wonderful eaten raw, or added to fruit salads, but lose much of their flavour if taken straight from the fridge.

Prunes are a healthy addition chopped into porridge, muesli or other breakfast cereals, but I think life's too short to stuff them with cream cheese, tasty though they may be.

Chicken breasts with raspberry and balsamic sauce

Any stir-fried meat goes well with a tart sauce. You could use apples or gooseberries, but I love the aromatic combination of raspberries and balsamic vinegar, and it's so simple and quick to do. Like all the recipes in this book of Superfoods, this one is as healthy as it is delicious.

BENEFITS

- This dish contains plenty of vitamin B6, phosphorus and selenium, and more than half a day's requirement of protein.

Serves 2

150g (5oz) fresh or frozen raspberries

200ml (7fl oz) red wine

1 tbsp runny honey

2 tbsp balsamic vinegar

2 tbsp peanut oil

2 skinless chicken breasts, sliced into thin strips crossways

1 clove garlic, crushed

2 spring onions, finely sliced lengthways

small piece fresh or preserved lemon grass

coarse sea salt and a few crushed black peppercorns

Put the raspberries into a saucepan and add the wine, honey and balsamic vinegar. Bring to a simmer and then set aside to rest – if it starts to thicken, reheat and stir.

Heat the oil in a wok or deep frying pan. Add the chicken, garlic, spring onions and lemon grass and stir vigorously over a high heat for 6 minutes. Season and serve with the hot sauce and your favourite salad.

Salmon with strawberry and tarragon dressing

Salmon simply oozes with health-giving nutrients (Pacific salmon are fattier than those caught in the Atlantic or Scotland, so contain more of the fat linked nutrients).

BENEFITS

- Salmon is rich in protein and a major source of omega-3 fats.
- It is an excellent source of vitamins B6 and B12, niacin and selenium.
- The dressing contains vitamin C and has a strong anti-inflammatory, cardio-protective effect.
- Each portion of this recipe can provide you with a whole day's supply of vitamin D.

Serves 4

4 salmon steaks

50g (2oz) unsalted butter

175g (6oz) strawberries, hulled

150ml (5fl oz) sunflower oil

1 tbsp sherry vinegar

small handful tarragon leaves, finely chopped

Season the salmon steaks. Put the butter into a large frying pan and fry the fish gently, skin side down, until half cooked. Remove the pan from the heat, turn the steaks over and leave them in the pan to finish cooking while you make the dressing.

In a food processor, mix together the strawberries, oil and vinegar. Pour into a bowl, add the tarragon and stir gently.

Serve the salmon hot, with the strawberry and tarragon dressing poured over.

TIP: The special flavour of tarragon helps bring out the sweet and sour properties of the strawberries, making this a perfect accompaniment to hot or cold poultry.

Duck and strawberry salad

This is a salad to die for – particularly in summer, when eating *al fresco* is on many people's minds. For a picnic, it's a doddle – as long as you keep it in a cold bag to prevent any risk of food poisoning. If you're doing Sunday lunch for friends, you can make this in the morning and then spend time getting ready. Forget slaving over the kitchen stove – you can just serve up this masterpiece of culinary art and Superfood good health.

Serves 4

2 duck breasts, with skin well scored

2 nests Chinese rice noodles

1 tbsp balsamic vinegar

1 tbsp extra-virgin olive oil

2 tbsp sesame seed oil

zest and juice of 1 lime

1 celery stalk, thinly sliced

4 spring onions, thinly sliced

1 handful washed watercress

225g (8oz) strawberries

2 ripe peaches, cut into 16 wedges

2 apricots, cut into 8 slices

In a hot frying pan, cook the duck until the skin is brown and crisp, turning once. Drain off and reserve excess fat. Leave to rest, then cut into thin slices. Cook the noodles according to packet instructions. Drain, let dry, then add to the hot pan with the duck fat and cook over a high heat until they are crisp. Whisk together the vinegar, oils, lime zest and juice. Stir in the celery and onions. Mound the noodles on the watercress, and pour on the dressing. Lay the sliced, warm duck across the middle and surround with fruit.

BENEFITS

- Duck is a good source of iron and B vitamins.
- Combining the meat with the high vitamin C content of the strawberries and lime juice will maximize the amount of iron you can absorb.
- Watercress provides protection from lung cancer.
- Peaches and apricots contain protective carotenoids.

Plaice with ginger, apples and red cabbage

Apples and red cabbage go together like the proverbial horse and carriage. Although most people will know this combination as an accompaniment to more robust winter food, here it assumes an altogether lighter flavour with one of my favourite fish, plaice. The recipe tastes just as good warm or cold.

BENEFITS

■ This combination of ingredients provides a mega-dose of heart, circulation and cancer-preventive nutrients.

■ The plaice gives you all the protein and selenium, and half the vitamin B12 that you need for a day.

Serves 4

2 tbsp rapeseed oil

2.5cm (1in) ginger root, peeled and finely chopped

½ large red cabbage, shredded

2 tbsp cider vinegar

2 tsp soft brown sugar

2 Granny Smith apples, cored and cut into slices

175g (6oz) unsalted butter

4 plaice fillets

300ml (10fl oz) milk

150g (5oz) fine breadcrumbs

3 tbsp fresh parsley leaves, finely chopped

Heat the oil in a large frying pan, add the ginger and cook until it's just beginning to give off its aroma – about 2 minutes.

Add the cabbage, turn down the heat, cover and cook until softened, stirring occasionally – about 15 minutes. Add the vinegar and sugar and continue cooking, stirring continuously, until the sugar is dissolved – about 5 minutes.

In another large pan, soften the apple slices in about 50g (2oz) of the butter (or cover with greaseproof paper and microwave on high for about a minute). Remove from the heat and keep warm.

While the cabbage is cooking, trim the plaice fillets – this is best done with a sharp pair of scissors – cutting them into 9cm (3½in) fingers, and soak in the milk.

In a wide, shallow dish, mix together the breadcrumbs and parsley. Take the fish out of the milk and dip into the mixture, making sure each piece is well covered.

Melt enough butter to cover the bottom of another frying pan and fry the fish until golden – about 3 minutes on each side. Drain on kitchen paper. If you need to fry in batches, keep warm until all the fish is cooked.

Arrange half the apple slices in the middle of a serving platter, top with the cabbage mixture, then the rest of the apple slices. Arrange the fish around the side.

Grilled figs with goat's cheese

If ever there were a Cinderella Superfood, it has to be figs. Fresh, they are the most succulent, sensuous, satisfying, sexy and sumptuous of fruits. Dried, they're a source of instant energy when you need that extra surge of physical or mental strength. This is one of the simplest and healthiest desserts – or, if you wish, serve it as a starter. Who cares? It's delicious whenever you eat it. The sweetness of the figs goes brilliantly with the slight sourness of the goat's cheese, and the honey gives it a wonderful golden glaze.

Serves 4

8 ripe fresh figs

225g (8oz) semi-hard goat's cheese – not one of the very soft spreadable varieties

runny honey for drizzling

Halve the figs lengthwise. Cut the goat's cheese into approximately 1cm (½in) slices, trimmed to fit on top of the figs. Put into an ovenproof dish. Heat the grill to its hottest. Put the figs and cheese under the grill for about 2 minutes, until the cheese is bubbling and golden. Drizzle over the honey to serve.

TIP: As an extra, sprinkle the figs with dry-fried sesame or pistachio nuts before drizzling over the honey.

BENEFITS

- Figs contain the anti-cancer agent benzaldehyde.
- They also contain healing enzymes, flavonoids and ficin, a natural chemical that starts the breakdown of proteins and improves digestion.
- Figs are a rich source of iron, potassium, betacarotene, fibre and energy.

Casserole of quail with apple and garlic

Quail has less fat than duck, and its flavour is more interesting than yet another chicken dish. Combined with the apple and nutrient-rich home-made chicken stock, you will be serving a hotpot of taste, pleasure and good health.

BENEFITS

- Thanks to the quail, each portion supplies all the protein and over half of the selenium, zinc, copper and iron you need each day.
- Garlic provides the heart and cancer protection and helps lower cholesterol.
- Apples contain the special fibre, pectin that helps reduce blood pressure. They are also a good source of vitamin C and are anti-inflammatory.

Serves 4

110g (4oz) unsalted butter

4 cloves garlic, finely chopped

4 quail

4 large cooking apples, or firm eating varieties, peeled, cored and quartered

1 tbsp runny honey

50ml (2fl oz) dry white wine

225ml (8fl oz) chicken stock

Preheat the oven to 220°C/425°F/gas 7.

Heat half the butter with the garlic in a large casserole dish – cast-iron if you have one – add the quails and cook on the hob, turning, until golden on all sides. Put in the oven for 15 minutes.

Meanwhile, sweat the apples gently in the rest of the butter. Add a little water, bring to the boil and simmer until just tender. Liquidize, then turn into a bowl and mix in the honey.

Take the quails out of the casserole, but keep hot. Deglaze the casserole with the wine, then add the chicken stock and boil for 2 minutes to reduce. Add the rest of the butter, cube by cube, stirring constantly, until emulsified.

Serve the quails with the sauce poured on top and the apple on the side.

Prawn and apple stir-fry

Stir-fries are a wonderful way of making a quick meal, even though the chopping takes time. This one is unusual because it contains apples, which give it a surprising piquancy; and the sauce, if I say so myself, is divine. But it's not just the taste that is so good. The Superfood complement of important nutrients, especially if ingredients come straight from your own garden, results in a meal for better growth, repair, strength and natural defences.

BENEFITS

- Apple, red pepper, mange touts and spring onions provide serious amounts of vitamin C, betacarotene, fibre and folic acid.
- Protein, omega-3 fats, iodine, zinc and selenium come from the prawns.

Serves 4

75ml (3fl oz) rapeseed oil

200g (7oz) king prawns, peeled weight

1 Golden Delicious apple, peeled, cored and thinly sliced

½ red pepper, cut into thin slithers lengthways

75g (3oz) mangetouts

4 thin spring onions, cut into 5cm (2in) lengths including the green part

3 tbsp brown sugar

1 tbsp cornflour

1 tbsp soy sauce

1 tsp ground ginger

rice or noodles to serve

Heat a third of the oil in a wok or a large, deep frying pan. Stir-fry the prawns until just turning golden. Remove with a slotted spoon into a warm bowl.

Using a little more oil if necessary, add the apple slices to the wok, stir-fry for 1 minute and put into the bowl with the prawns.

Pour another tablespoon of oil into the wok, add the pepper, mangetouts and spring onions and stir-fry for about 2 minutes. Add to the prawns and apples.

Mix together the sugar, cornflour, soy sauce and ground ginger with about 8 tablespoons of water. Stir until well combined. Pour into the wok and cook over a low heat, stirring continuously until thick. Tip in the rest of the ingredients and heat through. Serve with rice or noodles.

Honey and apricot pizza

Here is a sweet treat that is good for all the family and tastes terrific. Get the children to help with the preparation and they will tuck in with gusto when it comes to eating this change from the usual pizza napoletana.

BENEFITS

- This pizza provides energy, fibre, protein, calcium, betacarotene and vitamins C and E.

Serves 4

1 packet ready-made pizza dough

500g (1lb 2oz) fresh apricots

200g (7oz) low-fat crème fraîche

35g (1¼oz) sugar

1 tbsp runny honey

25g (1oz) pistachio nuts, unsalted

Preheat the oven to 200°C/400°F/gas 6. Place the dough on an oven tray covered with baking paper, and put it in the oven for 15–20 minutes.

Halve the apricots and remove the stones. Then cut the apricots into quarters. Whisk together the crème fraîche, sugar and honey, and spread the mixture onto the hot pizza dough, leaving a 2cm (¾in) outside border uncovered.

Add the apricot quarters in concentric circles. Sprinkle on the pistachios and return to the oven for around 20 minutes.

Allow to cool a little before serving up this delicious pudding or tea-time treat.

Berry quiche with feta and yogurt

This Superfood treat – delicious and good for you at the same time – is so simple to make, yet it looks as though a serious pastry cook has been at work. You can start from scratch and make the pastry yourself – or you can cheat and buy ready-made flan cases. What I do is use ready-made pastry to make the cases, which saves a great deal of time and effort and tastes pefectly fine. You can make one large quiche if you like (as shown here), but individual ones are no more work and look much nicer.

BENEFITS

- Feta and yogurt contain calcium.
- Blueberries and raspberries contain vitamins and antioxidants.

Serves 2

1 packet shortcrust pastry

200g (7oz) feta cheese

500g (1lb 2oz) 0% fat Greek yogurt

2 medium eggs

1 tbsp double cream

2 sprigs fresh mint leaves

1 tbsp fresh thyme – lemon thyme if possible

4 fresh basil leaves

freshly ground black pepper

125g (4oz) raspberries (usually 1 small punnet)

125g (4oz) strawberries (usually 1 small punnet)

220g (8oz) blueberries (usually 2 small punnets)

Preheat the oven to 180°C/350°F/gas 4. Grease two 15cm (6in) fluted quiche tins with removable bottoms.

Roll out the pastry, leaving it a bit thicker than you would do normally. Cut it about 2.5cm (1in) larger than the tins, and press it into them, working it round the circumference with your fingers. Brush with a little milk, cover with foil and bake in the oven until done – about 20 minutes.

In the meantime, put all the other ingredients except the fruit into a blender and whizz together into a nice thick, creamy paste. Fill each pastry case with the mixture, replace the foil and return to the oven for 20 minutes.

Remove the foil, add the fruit in circles and continue cooking until the mixture sets and begins to brown. Finish under a hot grill for a minute or two and enjoy.

TIP: You may not find lemon thyme in your local supermarket but you'll certainly find it at the garden centre. Why not buy a couple of plants for your herb garden? While you're there, you could also buy a pineapple sage plant and one or two of the more unusual mints, such as apple mint.

Raspberry bread and butter pudding

Forget what you remember from childhood days – this is indulgence, good health and Superfood on a plate. The tart taste of good British – or, even better, Scottish – raspberries gives this dessert a truly wonderful flavour. Frozen fruit will do if you can't find fresh but defrost it first. The pudding is just as tasty cold, but there is seldom any left over for the next day.

BENEFITS

- This recipe provides more than half of the vitamin C you need for one day, a third of the fibre and manganese, plus 12 per cent of the vitamin K, and that's just from the raspberries.
- Even more goodness comes from the calcium, protein, iron and B vitamins in the milk, eggs and bread.

Serves 4–6

110g (4oz) unsalted butter, ready to spread

8 thin slices of bread, crusts removed

350g (12oz) raspberries

450ml (16fl oz) double cream

200ml (7fl oz) milk

3 large free-range eggs

2 tbsp brandy

110g (4oz) caster sugar

Preheat the oven to 180°C/350°F/gas 4. Butter enough bread to cover the bottom of an ovenproof dish. Place it butter side down and scatter over half the raspberries.

Butter another layer of bread and place it butter side down on the fruit. Scatter over the rest of the raspberries, then add another layer of bread, again butter side down.

Mix together the cream and milk. Beat in the eggs, brandy and all but 1 tablespoon of the sugar. Pour the mixture over the bread and raspberries. Sprinkle the rest of the sugar on top and bake for about 30 minutes – until the top is crisp.

Blueberry tarts

These drop-dead-gorgeous, show-off tarts are simplicity itself. You'd pay a fortune for them at a smart deli, but you can make them at home in half an hour. I first got excited about blueberries in 1970 when I visited my cousin in the New England state of Maine. We took a boat on Moose Pond, a lake twice as big as Windermere, stopped for a picnic and went gathering wild blueberries. On the way back a storm got up and, having run out of petrol, we were blown, half full of water, on to a private beach. Luckily, the owner drove us back to our car. All the while, I held on to the bag of blueberries like grim death and my reward was a batch of these wonderful tarts.

Serves 4

1 sheet ready-made shortcrust pastry

60 fresh blueberries

2 free-range eggs

200ml (7fl oz) crème fraîche

2 level tbsp caster sugar

1 tsp vanilla essence

Preheat the oven to 200°C/400°F/gas 6. Butter four loose-bottomed 10cm (4in) flan tins and line them with the pastry. Arrange the blueberries on the bottom. Beat together the eggs, crème fraîche, sugar and vanilla essence. Pour over the berries and bake for 20 minutes.

BENEFITS

- Blueberries are a huge provider of anti-cancer phytochemicals as well as vitamins, minerals and fibre.

Gooseberry pudding

One of the advantages of the Superfood garden is the ability to grow your own special favourites and among mine are gooseberries. It is a shame that these berries are so underrated when they are so nutritious and versatile, just as good in savoury as in sweet dishes.

BENEFITS

- You can enjoy this dish without any feeling of pudding-guilt because you are getting all the heart benefit of the nuts and protein from the eggs – plus a grand dose of pleasure.
- Each portion contains 25 per cent of your day's fibre and almost a whole day's vitamin C.

Serves 4

175g (6oz) unsalted butter

75g (3oz) soft brown sugar

25g (1oz) chopped mixed nuts

350g (12oz) gooseberries, topped and tailed

110g (4oz) self-raising flour

2 pinches salt

110g (4oz) caster sugar

2 free-range eggs, beaten

Preheat the oven to 180°C/350°F/gas4.

Melt half the butter in a pan, add the brown sugar, stir well then add the nuts. Butter a deep ovenproof dish and pour in the mixture. Place the gooseberries on top.

Sieve together the flour and salt. Whisk the remaining butter with the caster sugar, add the eggs then the flour gradually, stirring well. Pour over the fruit and bake in the oven for 35 minutes.

When cooked, turn out onto a dish so that the gooseberries are on top.

Champagne berry jellies with mint cream

These may seem indulgent since they contain alcohol, sugar, cream and jelly, but it's not all bad news. After prunes, blueberries have the highest ORAC (oxygen radical absorbance capacity) score of all the fruits, and raspberries are not far behind. Orac units are the measurement of antioxidants in foods (see page 189). A little of what you fancy really can do you good!

BENEFITS

- Blueberries and raspberries are high in antioxidants.

Serves 4

6 large sprigs fresh mint

200ml (7fl oz) water

100g (3½oz) caster sugar

100ml (3½fl oz) champagne

juice of 1 lemon

10g (½oz) gelatine

110g (4oz) raspberries (usually 1 small punnet)

110g (4oz) blueberries (usually 1 small punnet)

175ml (6fl oz) single cream

½ tsp ground cinnamon

Put four of the mint sprigs into a saucepan with the water and 1 tablespoon of the sugar. Bring slowly to a simmer and leave to infuse and cool for 30 minutes. Then remove the mint.

Meanwhile, put the rest of the sugar in another pan with the champagne and simmer for 2 minutes. Add the lemon juice.

Dissolve the gelatine according to the packet instructions and add the champagne mixture.

Line four individual jelly moulds with clingfilm. Fill the bottom third of each mould with fruit. Pour in the gelatine and champagne syrup, and leave in the fridge to set for at least 3 hours.

To serve, stir the mint syrup into the cream and whisk until thick enough to form peaks. Place around the jellies, sprinkle with a pinch of cinnamon and decorate each one with a sprig of fresh mint.

TIP: The last time I made these, I managed to cut a small hole in the clingfilm of one mould and the jelly leaked through. It set under the film and was a messy disaster! Take care when cutting the film.

Baked quince with cinnamon and cloves

Most farms had a quince tree and a mulberry bush when I was a boy, growing up in rural England after the Second World War, and there was always a pot of quince jelly on the tea table to be eaten with cold pheasant, partridge or the best of English cheeses. Imagine my joy to find them again when I moved to France. A neighbour has a wonderful tree and brings a gift of a large box full each autumn. Quinces contain a lot of natural pectin so the cooking liquid will gel; they make fantastic jelly.

BENEFITS

■ Quinces contain precious quantities of antioxidant phytochemicals.

■ Cinnamon is an excellent anti-inflammatory, helps prevent blood clots and is great for diabetics because it regulates blood sugar levels.

■ Cloves contain eugenol, an oil that is used in temporary dental fillings for its pain-killing and antibacterial properties.

Serves 4

1.4kg (3lb) fresh quinces, washed thoroughly to remove the rough fuzz from the skin, halved and stem discarded

juice of ½ a lemon

350g (12oz) sugar

12 cloves

1 stick cinnamon

yogurt or cream for serving

Preheat the oven to 180°C/350°F/gas 4.

Remove the seeds from the quince halves, and the tough fibre surrounding the seeds, and set aside. Place the quince halves in a bowl of water combined with the lemon juice until ready to use, to prevent the fruit from darkening.

Put the quince seeds and fibre, the sugar and 250ml (9fl oz) water into a saucepan and boil for 10 minutes. Strain, reserving the liquid.

Push two cloves into each quince half and place the halves in a baking pan. Pour over the strained liquid, add the cinnamon and bake for 1½–2 hours, until the fruit is tender.

Serve warm or at room temperature with the thickened cooking liquid and yogurt or cream.

Cherry clafoutis

The cherries make this indulgent pudding good for you as well as delicious. Clafoutis started life as a speciality in France, where it was most popular in the Limousin region. Adding lemon balm not only gives a unique flavour, but also makes this dish calming and mood-enhancing.

BENEFITS

■ Cherries contain significant amounts of bioflavonoids and other plant chemicals, which puts them pretty near the top of the list of protective antioxidant foods. Their ellagic acid content adds to their anti-cancer properties.

■ Cherries are a reasonable source of vitamin C.

■ They contain plenty of potassium and virtually no sodium, so they're excellent for anyone with high blood pressure or heart disease.

■ Lemon balm protects against viral infection, particularly cold sores and other forms of herpes.

Serves 4

50g (2oz) unsalted butter

500g (1lb 2oz) cherries, stoned

1 tbsp lemon balm leaves, finely chopped

3 free-range eggs

50g (2oz) plain wholemeal flour, sifted

400ml (14fl oz) semi-skimmed milk

Grease a large, shallow, ovenproof dish with a little of the butter. Put the cherries into the dish with the lemon balm leaves.

Melt the rest of the butter gently and whisk it into the eggs. Now whisk in the flour and milk. Pour the egg mixture over the cherries and bake until set – about 45 minutes.

Plums poached in red wine

Like all the purple, blue-black and red fruits, dark-coloured plums are Superfoods because of their high content of antioxidants, the most effective protectors of the heart and vascular system and conveyors of anticancer chemicals that nature provides. Keep some of this fabulous dessert for breakfast, to serve over muesli for the best possible start to your day.

Serves 4

175g (6oz) brown caster sugar

350ml (12fl oz) red wine

75g (3oz) unsalted butter

450g (1lb) fresh, dark red plums (stoned weight)

yogurt or crème fraîche to serve

Put the sugar and wine into a wide saucepan and bring slowly to the boil, stirring constantly until the sugar is completely dissolved. Add the butter and stir well until it has melted. Add the plums carefully, cut side down. Simmer gently until just tender – about 15 minutes depending on size. Serve with yogurt or crème fraîche.

BENEFITS

■ Dark-coloured plums are a very rich source of powerful antioxidants.

■ All plums are a good source of vitamin C and contain vitamins A and K, as well as small quantities of minerals.

Pear pain perdu

An indulgence once in a while is good for the soul, and what you do most of the time is important, not the things you do once in a while. So there is no point in feeling guilty as this dessert vanishes spoonful by spoonful. Just savour it! Anyway, at least it makes up for the sugar and ice cream with some health-giving benefits. Pears are surprisingly good for you and are one of the least likely of all foods to cause allergic reactions. Dutch spice cake is like gingerbread and can generally be found in supermarkets.

Serves 6

275g (10oz) sugar
500ml (18fl oz) water
1 cinnamon stick
1 star anise
6 firm pears
4 slices Dutch spice cake
ice cream, to serve

Mix the sugar and water in a saucepan and bring to the boil. Break the cinnamon in bits and add to the water with the star anise. Simmer for 10 minutes.

Peel and halve the pears, leaving the stalk on. Add the pears to the saucepan, reduce heat to a minimum and cook for 30 minutes, basting a few times with the syrup. Crumble the cake, sprinkle it on the pears and cook for a further 10 minutes. Remove the pan from the heat and leave to cool.

Serve in bowls, drizzled with the syrup and accompanied by vanilla ice cream.

BENEFITS

■ Pears are an excellent source of pectin, the soluble fibre that helps to lower cholesterol and improve digestion. They also contain vitamins and minerals.

■ The cinnamon and nutmeg in the spice cake aid digestion and are mood-soothing.

chapter 9
herbs

choosing herbs • growing herbs •
what to do with your harvest

Choosing herbs

Many people are rediscovering the taste and health benefits of herbs. Their use is a culinary art that dates back to the Middle Ages and beyond. Residues of herbs have been found in prehistoric cave dwellings and the Pharaohs' tombs. Growing your own is not only easy but hugely satisfying, and whether you cultivate a herb garden or a few pots and hanging baskets on a balcony, you will be practising an age-old skill.

You can buy most herbs as plants from nurseries and garden centres, but some are actually better grown from seed. Annuals and biennials – basil, borage, dill, fennel, parsley and savory for example – are all better when you start from scratch. Nearly all can be sown in mid- to late spring, but some of the less hardy ones shouldn't be sown until there is no longer any risk of frost.

If you have a garden, plant your favourites as close to the kitchen door as you can. There is no sense in putting them at the bottom of the garden so you have to dash out in the rain, snow or sleet to get a few sage leaves for the Christmas turkey. Planting your herbs near the kitchen means you get not only the full flavour but also maximum medicinal benefit from the volatile oils and other active constituents, which start to degrade as soon as the herbs are harvested.

Nearly all the herb flowers are edible and taste good. Garlic, chive and garlic chive flowers are an attractive, flavour-enhancing addition to salads. Borage, lovage, mint and nasturtium flowers can all be frozen in ice cubes and then used to add to drinks or soups.

PRETTY TASTY

The flowers of many herbs are also both health-giving and delicious. Garlic, chives, lavender, sage, hyssop, camomile, rocket, nasturtiums and pinks are some of the most popular to bear in mind.

Containers

Be imaginative in your choice of containers – I've used old stone jars, cast-iron water troughs and old watering cans. The stainless steel drum from an old washing machine looks great in a modern setting and, of course, will last for many years. Anything that is an interesting shape will look good when full of herbs.

To produce the best results from container growing, good drainage is essential. Drill holes if necessary, and cover them with a substantial layer of broken pots or fine wire mesh. Stand your containers on stones or bricks to encourage drainage in the summer time and prevent waterlogging and frost damage in the winter. This ploy also helps to keep snails and slugs at bay.

Most herbs will thrive in a soil depth of about 30cm (12in), and the smaller varieties will grow happily in a 20cm (8in) deep window box. Naturally, bay trees and the shrubby bushes sage and rosemary will need much larger pots if they are to flourish and last for years. Be careful to work out the final height of a plant before selecting its pot so that the taller varieties don't become unstable and fall over.

SEASONAL TASKS

SPRING

Repot your herbs if the roots are coming through the bottom of the pot or the plant has obviously grown too large for the container. Lift the herb from the old pot, complete with soil and root ball, and place it in one at least a couple of sizes larger. Fill the spaces with the planting mixture, firm in and water well.

SUMMER

Deadhead and cut back any straggling growth. Don't forget to water every day even if it rains – not much rainwater will get into the pot.

AUTUMN

Cut back the perennials to stop them getting leggy, the gardening term for lots of bare woody stems with leaves on the end. If you skimp on this, the plant will produce far less of the bits you want to use when next summer comes around – and leggy herbs look awful, so don't be timid with the secateurs.

WINTER

Even hardy pot plants need protection from severe frosts. Covering them with horticultural fleece not only protects the plants but the pots too – a necessary precaution, as I've found to my cost. Terracotta pots sold as able to withstand frost may still crack if it gets very cold.

It really is a good idea to move your containers under cover for the worst of the winter – put them in a shed, garage, conservatory or any sheltered space. Consider placing your seriously heavy pots on wheeled bases so they are easier to move. Water very occasionally, using the bare minimum needed to keep the soil from drying out completely.

After four or five years you will need to change the compost completely in the bigger containers, but window boxes, hanging baskets and small pots will need changing annually. You will find a wide selection of suitable ready-made composts in your local garden centre. All containers and baskets need regular watering daily, possibly twice a day if it is very hot. I use a liquid seaweed feed added to the watering can, once a fortnight in the growing season.

Growing herbs

The beauty of growing your own herbs is that you can choose the ones you like the best and find most useful. With a plentiful supply, you can discover their versatility and the freshness of the flavours when used straight from the growing plant.

BASIL

Gardening: Grow this wonderful aromatic plant from seed in paper or fibre pots, not seed trays. Basil will do best if the long roots are not disturbed, so once the plant has grown enough to handle comfortably, and the risk of frost has passed, plant directly into the ground or container and water in well. Avoid evening watering because it's not happy with wet feet overnight. Basil is susceptible to mildew so give plants plenty of space for air to circulate, and sow seed thinly. The more you pick the leaves, the better it is as the plant will bush out and you will prevent flowering, although I like to let at least one pot flower to attract bees.

Eating: Basil is the main ingredient in pesto sauce, and a perfect match for tomatoes. Sweet basil is the most widely used with good-sized leaves and excellent taste. Purple basil is strongly scented, and the ball-shaped Greek basil produces the tiniest of all the basil leaves. Use them whole, sprinkled on tomatoes, salads and sauces.

BORAGE

Gardening: This stunning purple-flowered herb will thrive in poor soil or in a large pot. Grow from seed planted in mid- and late spring for a summer-long supply of young leaves and flowers. This is one of the best companion plants because it attracts lots of bees to pollinate the rest of your garden

If you want to encourage more growth, remove flower heads as soon as they appear. Do not throw them away as many are good to eat so add to recipes, fruit dishes and salads.

and is a favourite of the blackfly, thus keeping them away from your beans.

Eating: The leaves feel hairy, but try them finely sliced in salads, mixed with mayonnaise, crème fraîche or natural yogurt. Add the flowers to drinks and sweet and savoury dishes.

CHERVIL

Gardening: Sow seed in spring and autumn – chervil will stand the winter with a modicum of protection, but avoid full sun, which will make the small white flowers appear too soon. The pale green leaves can take on a purple tinge by the end of summer, but they still taste good.

Eating: The subtle hint of aniseed is fantastic combined with most vegetables, poultry, white fish, soups and stocks.

CHIVES

See pages 42–43.

CORIANDER

Gardening: Sow successively from early spring to late autumn. Use the lower leaves first, then the smaller, stronger upper ones. Coriander hates having wet feet, so water sparingly and in the morning so the sun can do its job. Once flowered, the seeds will soon ripen and can be collected by hanging flowering stems upside down in a paper bag.

Eating: Leaves and seeds have very different tastes and aromas.

DILL

Gardening: Grow from seed planted in situ from mid- to late spring, or in small plug pots in a heated propagator much earlier. It does well in poor soil and full sun, and is fine in a container. It needs a fairly large pot in a light airy spot, out of the midday sun. Unless you pick it regularly, the plant will grow tall and untidy and stop producing fine leaves.

Eating: Dill's fine leaves are used in many fish recipes. The seeds are good in rice dishes and meat stews and are famously used in dill pickles, gravlax and pickled herrings.

Medicinal: Dill alleviates indigestion, colic and wind, and is the main ingredient in babies' gripe water.

FENNEL

Gardening: Both green and bronze varieties can be sown directly into the ground or in good-sized pots, but don't plant if there is a risk of frost, and protect from midday sun. Fennel is a good companion plant, attracting lots of butterflies, but keep it away from dill or coriander as they may cross-pollinate. Once established, this perennial will make a bushy clump that lasts for three or four years.

Eating: Fennel is fabulous with fish, salads, soups, sauces and in vegetable quiches.

Medicinal: 5g (1 teaspoon) of fennel seeds in a mug of boiling water, covered and left to stand for ten minutes, is an excellent remedy for indigestion, flatulence and heartburn.

HORSERADISH

Gardening: This pungent root is simple to grow. Horseradish does well in just about any soil and anywhere. Lengths of root, known as 'slips', can be bought from specialist plant suppliers, but if you know where it grows, ask permission to dig up a root or two in the autumn. Cut the root into 20cm (8in) lengths and plant where you want your

The Romans brought many herbs to Britain, and often grew them in circular gardens. I found an old seed-sowing machine at a farm sale many years ago, and used one of the wheels as my herb planter. The spaces between the spokes make perfect dividers to separate the different plants.

clump to grow, but beware – horseradish can take over your garden. Keep it in an isolated spot or bury an old dustbin with plenty of drainage holes in the bottom, fill with soil and plant the slips inside to stop it spreading.

Eating: Strongest when fresh, horseradish root is wonderful as an accompaniment to all smoked fish, as well as roast beef. Add the young leaves to a piquant salad.

Medicinal: A powerful antiseptic, circulation stimulant and clearer of nose and sinuses.

LEMON BALM

Gardening: Buy as a small plant or sow seeds in spring directly into the soil. This perennial is hardy and can be divided into several clumps in the winter. It makes a biggish shrub, so needs space or a large pot. Lemon balm is very attractive to bees, so every other plant will get better pollination.

Eating: Lemon balm tastes delicious, so long as you don't try to cook it! Fresh leaves torn onto a salad, or mixed with soft cheese, fish and alcoholic cold fruit cups add a hint of citrus, but without the acidity of real lemons.

Medicinal: A powerful medicinal herb, this plant has antiviral properties. At the first sign of a cold sore, crush a leaf and rub on the affected area and it may stop developing. Make a tea with 1 teaspoon of chopped leaves in a cup of boiling water. Cover, stand for ten minutes, then chill and keep in the fridge for up to ten days. Dab on cold sores three times a day for rapid relief.

MINT

Gardening: If you grow just one herb, choose one of the many varieties of mint. Buy plants from a specialist herb grower to make sure you get true varieties, which is often not the case with seed. Mints like rich damp soil, so don't let them dry out. They can be very invasive – growing them in an old bucket with the bottom knocked out will keep them under control. Mint can be propagated by dividing clumps or from root cuttings, but take care as any portion of root that gets left or scattered will soon produce a crop of shoots along its length.

Eating: With care, you can enjoy fresh mint in salads and sauces through the winter months. Apple, ginger, pineapple, basil and lemon mints are all delicious. Among my favourites are spearmint (for sauces, jellies and juleps) and Moroccan mint – the best for refreshing mint tea and to use in North African and Middle Eastern salads.

Medicinal: Peppermint (a hardy perennial that will spread all over your garden if you don't control it) is a strong and effective antacid. Its essential oil, menthol, is an ingredient in many indigestion remedies. Eau de Cologne mint is a fantastic aromatic herb to add to your bath or shower. Tie a generous handful of leaves in a muslin square and hang under the tap or use as a sponge to invigorate and relieve headaches.

PARSLEY

Gardening: Sow the seed ofr this biennial in early spring, either in the ground or in pots. Germinate under cover or in a heated propagator and plant out when there is no risk of frost. With early and late sowings, you can have parsley all year round. Parsley needs rich, well-fed soil. Water during hot weather and cut regularly to prevent flowering. In cold climates, protect the plants during autumn and winter.

Eating: The main varieties are curly-leaved

The seeds of dill, caraway, mustard and the fennels are very useful in cooking and preserving. When these plants have flowered and start going to seed, cut them down, keeping long stems and taking care not to shake off the seeds. See page 185 for drying instructions.

and flat-leaved (the latter has a better flavour and is used more in cooking). Full of flavour and rich in calcium and betacarotene, this is a plant that we should eat in abundance.
Medicinal: A genuine breath freshener.

PENNYROYAL

Gardening: Perfect for a container, this grows well from seed. Once established, it is a hardy perennial, although it may need some winter protection. Semi-evergreen with pretty flowers, it is a powerful insect repellent, and I have a pot outside the kitchen door to deter ants. Its name comes from the Latin word for flea, *pulga*, and pennyroyal tied in muslin bags makes a natural flea repellent, if you have animals in the house.
Eating: Use pennyroyal like other members of the mint family, but bear in mind that its constituents are rather different, giving it a strong peppermint flavour, so use sparingly.
Medicinal: A weak infusion is excellent for colds. Use for headaches associated with nausea, migraine and travel sickness, and to help improve digestion.

ROCKET

Gardening: Grow from seed planted directly into the soil from spring through to autumn, or even winter in warm, sheltered places. Pick often to stop flowering and bolting.
Eating: You will be eating the tender young leaves in salads in around a couple of months from sowing. As they age, the peppery taste becomes more pronounced.

ROSEMARY

Gardening: There are many varieties, but *Rosmarinus officinalis* is the most widely used as it lasts for years, looks good, tastes great, is seldom attacked by pests and is simple to look after. Grow from cuttings – it's tricky from seed. Equally happy in a pot or in the ground, it likes well-drained, warm, sheltered positions. With luck it will flower twice, but apart from a gentle tidy-up, do not prune until all frost risk has passed. If the shrub starts getting leggy with lots of bare woody stems, cut it back hard in mid-spring to get back to a good shape. The bush will need some protection with fleece if temperatures fall much below freezing.
Eating: Often used to flavour roast lamb, rosemary also goes well with most other meats and poultry. It is excellent added to flavoured oils (see page 186).
Medicinal: This herb is traditionally said to improve memory, which is why you see it so often in gardens of remembrance.

SAGE

Gardening: Common sage and purple sage are hardy perennial evergreens that will give you leaves throughout the year, as well as attractive, tasty flowers in summer. Both types will grow from seed but starting with a couple of plants is easier. Keep in good shape by pruning in early to late spring, depending on climate, and then again after summer flowering. Don't cut back in autumn if your winters are cold and frosty. Save hard cutting back for springtime.
Eating: Traditionally used in pork stuffing, cooked with liver and added to soups and casseroles, sage also gives delicious flavour to vegetable dishes, used sparingly. One remarkable thing about sage is the way it helps the digestion of fats. It works a bit like washing-up liquid as it helps to break down the fats into tiny globules and creates a

Old Wives' Tale?
When I lived in a tiny English village, I had help from a real country 'old boy', who was fond of garden lore and superstition. Mr Barwick used to say that parsley was the devil's herb and would thrive only if the seed was planted on Good Friday. I don't know how true this is, but I have always followed his advice and never had a failure with parsley. Coincidence?

larger surface area for the gastric juices to work on. It's no coincidence that sage is traditionally added to high fat foods, such as pork, liver and sausages.

Medicinal: Thanks to its powerful antiseptic essential oils, sage helps protect against infections. For a sore throat, add 2 teaspoons of fresh, chopped leaves to a cup of boiling water, cover and leave for ten minutes. When cool, use as a gargle – swill each mouthful around the back of the throat, then spit out, or swallow if you like the taste. Repeat every three hours.

SUMMER SAVORY

Gardening: Plant in a medium-sized pot after germinating the seed in uncovered trays. It is a half-hardy annual and needs some protection from frost, and constant picking of the leaves to prevent flowering.

Eating: Savory is used in most salamis, and you can add it to any bean dish, such as chilli, chickpea casserole and bean salads.

Medicinal: If you like to eat beans, you should grow summer savory. In fact, it is called the bean herb in some parts of Europe because it helps prevent the flatulence that follows any meal containing dried, canned or even fresh beans.

TARRAGON

Gardening: French tarragon has a far better flavour than Russian tarragon but is hard to grow from seed, so buy plants from a specialist dealer. Grown in the ground or in pots, tarragon will be fine for around three years. After that, it loses some of its unique taste. Root cuttings can be taken in the frost-free mid- to late spring. Plant sections as long as your middle finger in pots and

keep covered in a warm spot. Once rooted, harden off for ten days before planting out.

Eating: Fabulous with rice, salads, tomatoes, fish, beef and chicken. This is the herb that gives béarnaise sauce its distinctive flavour.

THYME

Gardening: There are many varieties but the most useful is common thyme. Buy a plant and propagate by cuttings to ensure you keep the true plant. A hardy perennial with pale mauve flowers, it needs poor, well-drained soil, so unless you have very sandy ground, use pots. I grow three or four in separate containers and take plenty of cuttings. Keep cuttings in a sheltered spot over winter and protect against frosts.

Eating: Thyme is the perfect match for chicken and oily fish, and goes well in all soups, stews and casseroles. As a vital part of bouquet garni, it is used in most stocks.

Medicinal: Used to protect against infections since the time of the Pharaohs, thyme's antiseptic qualities are still valued. Thyme tea is an excellent mouthwash and good for infected gums and mouth ulcers. In fact, the pink liquid the dentist asks you to rinse your mouth with contains thymol – an antiseptic originally extracted from thyme.

There are many varieties of sage, the most popular being the green, purple, variegated and pineapple sages. They all do well in pots and will benefit from a bit of protection and warmth in very cold climates. Keep close to the kitchen door as these leaves, and the flowers, are best picked as you need them. Use sparingly in soups, salads, risotto and with any liver recipe.

What to do with your harvest

So long as you are prepared to take some time and trouble, your own home-grown herbs will always be better, with more taste and smell, than any you can buy – and it's easy to dry or freeze them for use when fresh plants are not available.

Drying

Some of the best herbs for drying are dill, tarragon, bay, oregano, rosemary, sage and thyme. Fennel and coriander seeds and juniper berries also dry well. In general, the more you cut from your herb plants, the more vigorous their growth.

The strongest concentration of smell and taste occurs just before flowering, so this is when to gather your herbs. Collect them early on a sunny morning, after dew has evaporated and before the heat of the sun sweats out the volatile oils. Take 7.5cm (3in) sprigs rather than separate leaves, and use a very sharp knife or scissors to avoid bruising and loss of flavour.

Quick drying gives you the best flavour and that requires plenty of circulating air and moderate heat. Temperatures between 21°C (70°F) and 38°C (100°F) will suit most herbs – an airing cupboard with the door slightly ajar, a warm, dark loft (cover any skylight windows) or an oven at a very low temperature with the door not quite shut.

Lay the herbs on a muslin-covered rack, keeping the varieties separate, and turn two or three times a day for the first 48 hours; or hang them in small bunches. When the leaves become brittle, they are ready. Rub them into small pieces, taking care not to overdo it or you'll end up with herb powder.

Collect seeds by tying a paper bag (not plastic as it sweats) over the flower heads

TIP
When using your dried herbs, remember that they are much more strongly flavoured than their fresh originals, so be sparing. A teaspoon of any dried leaf produces the same intensity of flavour as a tablespoon of the chopped fresh plant.

and hanging from the stems until the seeds have dropped. Lay them out for drying, which may take 10–14 days.

Store dried herbs and seeds in airtight, screw-top, dark glass jars. Moisture and sunlight will quickly spoil the quality. Do not use plastic containers as they tend to sweat, which encourages mildew.

Freezing

Herbs that freeze brilliantly are chives, chervil, tarragon, coriander, lemon balm, mint, basil, parsley, sorrel and savory. One of the benefits of freezing is that the vivid colours and flavours are preserved. It's quick and there's no need for blanching. Wrap herbs in plastic bags before freezing, as their strong aromas can easily permeate other food. Once individual bags are frozen, store in freezer containers as double protection against physical damage. There's no need to thaw herbs before use.

I like to freeze some herbs into ice cubes. Finely chop parsley, chives or tarragon and put a couple of teaspoons in each ice-cube compartment, fill with water and freeze. When frozen, empty the cubes into labelled bags and add directly to recipes.

Herb oils

No matter whether you are preparing savoury or sweet oils, the method is identical, but the type of oil used varies.

- Extra virgin olive oil – for salad dressings, marinades, pasta, rice, grills, barbecues and dishes that don't need prolonged or very hot frying.
- Rapeseed oil – the healthiest oil for frying because it has the ideal balance of omega-3 and omega-6 fatty acids, or peanut oil for dishes that need prolonged or deep-frying.
- Cold-pressed grapeseed or almond oil – for sweet dishes, especially good for marinating fruit.

The method is the same for all herbal oils. Flavouring is a matter of personal taste, so all quantities are approximate and variable to suit your own palate. It's best to make small quantities so that your oils are used before they go rancid, which all oil does in time. Unless made with old oil, these health-giving mixtures will keep for six months. Keep in dark-coloured bottles, or cover the bottle with foil, and store in a cool place out of sunlight, but not in the fridge.

- Use garlic, basil or tarragon singly as savoury oils.
- Lavender, scented geraniums, rose petals or mint are good for sweet oils.
- A combination of thyme, sage, garlic and coriander is great in marinades for chicken, lamb, pork and shellfish.
- Coriander, fennel, tarragon, oregano, parsley, dill, sweet marjoram, lemon thyme, southernwood and bergamot all make good oils on their own or in combinations.
- For stir-frying, add garlic, coriander, dried citrus peel, basil and lemongrass to sesame, walnut or pistachio oils.

Herb vinegars

These vinegars are superb time-savers – you can add the taste of herbs without having to gather, wash or prepare them. They are perfect for salad dressings, vinaigrettes or marinades and added sparingly to gravies and sauces. I prefer them made with single herbs and always use the best-quality cider or white wine varieties.

As for oils, the basic method is the same whatever herbs you are using. Decant the vinegar into a bottle with a largish neck and an airtight stopper. Wash your leaves, petals or seeds if necessary and dry thoroughly. Bruise gently in a mortar or with the back of a wooden spoon (partially crush seeds). Put the herbs in the vinegar, stopper tightly and leave for three weeks before using.

These vinegars will keep for months – just make sure the herbs are always covered with vinegar by topping up the bottles. When the flavour starts to fade, strain the remaining vinegar into another bottle and start again.

ROSEMARY OIL

250ml (9fl oz) oil
1 tbsp fresh rosemary leaves

Put the leaves in a mortar with a little of the oil and pound gently to release flavours. Add to the rest of the oil and pour into a tight-fitting screw-top jar. Leave on a sunny windowsill for three weeks, shaking gently every day or so. Strain through muslin and pour into any bottle with a screw top or flip top (like old-fashioned lemonade bottles), a tight-fitting stopper or cork. Finish by adding a sprig of fresh rosemary. Use with lamb or poultry and with pasta salads.

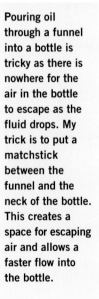

Pouring oil through a funnel into a bottle is tricky as there is nowhere for the air in the bottle to escape as the fluid drops. My trick is to put a matchstick between the funnel and the neck of the bottle. This creates a space for escaping air and allows a faster flow into the bottle.

Vital vitamins and essential minerals

The amount of each vitamin that the average person requires per day is known as the Reference Nutrient Intake (RNI), so here then is a list of what the most important vitamins do, the RNI and how much you have to eat to get that amount from your food. Measurements are usually in milligrams (mg) or micrograms (µg) – one microgram is the same as one thousandth of a milligram.

Vitamin A
RNI 800µg
Essential for growth, skin, night and colour vision.

RNI from one of these:
5g (1 tsp) of liver, 40g (1½oz) of old carrots, 70g (2½oz) of spinach, butter or margarine, 120g (4¼oz) of broccoli with 60g (2oz) of Cheddar cheese in a sauce.

Vitamin C
RNI 60mg
Aim for at least 500mg
Prevents scurvy, aids wound healing and iron absorption, and is a vital antioxidant. This is a powerful heart protective, anti-cancer vitamin and I believe you certainly need at least 500mg a day for optimum health.

RNI from one of these:
a dessertspoon of blackcurrants, a lemon, half a green pepper, an orange, half a large grapefruit, a kiwi fruit, 90g (3oz) of raw red cabbage.

Vitamin D
RNI 10µg
Aim for 15µg
Essential for bone formation, because it is part of the calcium absorption system. Lack of this vitamin causes rickets in children and bone disorders in adults. The action of ultraviolet light on the skin produces vitamin D. Those at special risk of deficiency are the elderly and other groups who get little fresh air and daylight exposure. The Asian community is often at risk due to traditional clothing, diet and lifestyle.

RNI from one of these:
1 teaspoon of cod liver oil, 45g (1½oz) of herring or kipper, 55g (2oz) of mackerel, 80g (2¾ oz) of canned salmon or tuna, 135g (4¾ oz) of canned sardines. Eggs and margarine are fair sources, too.

Vitamin B1 (thiamin)
RNI 1.4mg
Aim for 5mg
Main function is to aid the conversion of carbohydrates into energy. If you live on a high-starch diet – some vegetarians do – or drink a lot of alcohol, the need for B1 increases. It's also essential for transmitting nerve impulses between the brain and spinal cord. For optimum health, go for 5mg.

RNI from one of these:
60g (2oz) of cod roe, 70g (2½oz) of wheatgerm, 100g (3½oz) of brazil or peanuts. Oatmeal, bacon, pork, offal and bread are all good sources, too.

Vitamin B2 (riboflavin)
RNI 1.6mg
Aim for 2mg
Vital for growth and for healthy skin, hair, nails and mucous membranes. For peak protection, aim for 2mg a day.

RNI from one of these:
6 eggs, 850ml (1½ pints) of milk, 65g (2¼oz) of liver or kidney, 250g (9oz) cheddar cheese. Beef, mackerel, almonds, cereals and poultry are also good sources.

Vitamin B3 (niacin)
RNI 18mg
Aim for 25mg
Required to manufacture the enzymes that release energy from your food during digestion. It's also valuable for skin and nerve tissue. For peak protection, aim for 25mg daily.

RNI from one of these:
150g (5oz) of roast chicken, 200g (7oz) beef, 2 boiled eggs with 2 slices of wholemeal toast.

Vitamin B5 (pantathenic acid)
RNI 6mg
Aim for 20mg
Important for conversion of fat and sugar into energy, and for the production of antibodies that protect against infection. For peak protection, aim for 20mg daily.

RNI from one of these:
100g (3½oz) liver, 1 avocado, 2 handfuls of unsalted peanuts. Useful amounts are contained in eggs, oats, pulses, poultry and dried fruits. Significant amounts are produced by natural bacteria in the intestine.

Vitamin B6 (pyridoxine)
RNI 2mg
Aim for 50mg daily
Essential for growth because it's needed to make and mend muscle tissue. Many women have found it helpful in the treatment of the symptoms of PMS, and it may overcome some of the side effects of the contraceptive pill. For peak protection, aim for 50mg each day.

RNI from one of these:
1 large banana, half an avocado. Fish, meat, liver and cheese are good sources. A portion of cod or salmon, or a grilled herring will give you almost the RNI.

Vitamin B12
RNI 1.5µg
Aim for 5µg
Vital to prevent anaemia and essential for healthy red blood cells and the transmission of nerve impulses. Deficiency may be a problem for vegetarians and especially vegans.

RNI from one of these:
50g (2oz) of beef, 1 egg, a portion of cod, a couple of mouthfuls of liver.

Vitamin E
RNI 10mg
Aim for 50mg
Long thought to be required for fertility but now known to be a powerful antioxidant that protects against heart disease and cancer. Also important for healthy skin.

RNI from one of these:
2 tablespoons of sunflower seeds, 2 teaspoons of wheatgerm oil, 5 teaspoons of sunflower oil, 50g (2oz) of hazelnuts or almonds. Olive oil, avocado, spinach and other nuts and seeds are all good sources.

Folic acid
RNI 200µg
Aim for 400µg Vital during growth and development and essential for all women of childbearing age because birth defects are linked directly to deficiency. It's also now known that low levels are an important cause of heart disease.

RNI from one of these:
75g (3oz) of liver, 80g (2¾oz) of fortified breakfast cereal, 100g (3½oz) of Brussels sprouts, 100g (3½oz) of spinach. Other good sources are all dark green vegetables, kidney, nuts, wholemeal bread, frozen peas, chick peas and raw red cabbage.

Vitamin K
no RNI
Essential as part of the blood-clotting mechanism. This nutrient is manufactured by probiotic bacteria during digestion, and is given to new babies at birth. Few people need extra supplies other than those with bowel diseases who may not absorb sufficient amounts, or women with very heavy periods.

Get vitamin K from: all green vegetables.

Essential minerals

Your body needs these magic minerals – some in tiny amounts, others in intermediate amounts and a few in minute traces. They're all essential and missing out on any, even the trace minerals, can make the difference between health and sickness. For example, a breastfeeding mum needs 1,000–1,500mg of calcium each day, 15mg of iron and 75µg of selenium.

Zinc
RNI 15mg

Vital for growth, wound healing, healthy sex organs, reproduction, insulin production and natural resistance. Lack of zinc can lead to weight loss, skin diseases, ulcers and acne, lower sex-drive, loss of taste and smell, and brittle nails. Too much will reduce the copper in the body.

Zinc deficiency can be a factor in so many conditions that it is a mineral I'm always on the look-out for. Take care if you're a vegetarian or vegan, or are constantly on weight-reducing diets. It is vital for healthy sperm, male sexual performance and protection of the prostate gland.

RNI from one of these: 25g (1oz) of oysters, 90g (3oz) of wheatgerm, 200g (7oz) of calves' liver, 300g (10oz) of pumpkin seeds or 100g (3½oz) of sardines + 250g (9oz) of shellfish. Other good sources are lamb, steak, garlic, ginger root, Brazil nuts, eggs, oats, crab, almonds and chicken. But don't eat vast quantities of bran, since this can stop the zinc from being absorbed by the body.

Selenium
No RNI

Advised minimum daily intake 70µg

Part of the self-defence system, important for cholesterol control and vital for protection against heart disease and prostate cancer. Deficiencies may lead to low resistance, heart disease and skin problems.

American studies have shown that where the soil is richest in selenium, the number of people who get cancer is 20 per cent lower than in parts of the country that have soil poor in selenium. Prostate and breast cancers are specifically linked to low selenium consumption.

Get advised daily amount from: 5g (1 teaspoon) of shelled Brazil nuts, 10g (½oz) of mixed nuts and raisins, 45g (1½oz) of fresh tuna, 3 slices of wholemeal bread made with American or Canadian wheat, 50g (2oz) of shrimps + 50g (2oz) of sunflower seeds + 50g (2oz) of plaice stir-fried together in a wok. Other good sources are butter, oily fish, liver and kidney.

Iron
RNI 14mg

Combines with oxygen to make haemoglobin, the red colouring of the blood. This transports the air you breathe to every cell of the body. Without enough of it, you will get anaemia, fatigue, depression and palpitations, and you will look pale. Too much can lower your natural resistance and cause insomnia, tiredness and depression.

Spinach is not much use for iron because it contains oxalic acid, which prevents it from being absorbed. The tannin in tea also interferes with iron absorption and is a factor in anaemia. Bran can cause problems, too, but vitamin C taken at the same time as cereals improves iron uptake.

RNI from one of these: 150–200g (5–7oz) of liver, 200g (7oz) of roast pheasant, 75g (3oz) of pigeon, 75g (3oz) of black pudding or a medium-sized steak, 6 fresh dates + a handful of mixed fresh nuts and raisins. Other good sources are kelp (seaweed), molasses, kidneys, beef, pilchards, kidney beans, Brazil nuts, lentils, peanuts, chicken, soya beans and peas.

Copper
No RNI

Advised minimum daily intake 1.2mg.

Works with iron to make red blood corpuscles, and is important for bone formation, breakdown of cholesterol and the skin pigment melanin.

Get advised daily amount from: 15g (1 tablespoon) of calves' liver, 3 oysters, 2 crab sandwiches, 1 wholemeal sardine sandwich + a handful of fresh unsalted peanuts. Other good sources are lamb, mushrooms, shellfish, nuts, wholemeal bread, butter, barley and olive oil.

Calcium
RNI 800mg

Aim for 1,000–1,500mg if you're pregnant or breastfeeding

Vital for the formation and continuing strength of bones. You need vitamin D to enable your body to utilize calcium, so make sure you eat plenty of oily fish and get sensible exposure to sunlight, which helps the body make its own.

RNI from one of these: a glass of milk + a carton of yoghurt + 50g (2oz) of cheese; 100g (3½oz) of tinned sardines with the bones + 100g (3½oz) of dried figs; 100g (3½oz) of muesli with milk; 100g (3½oz) of tofu stir-fried with 100g (3½oz) of green beans and 50g (2oz) of sesame seeds. Other good sources are dried fruits, sprats, whitebait, nuts, seeds and green vegetables.

Potassium
No RNI

Advised minimum daily intake 3,500mg

Essential for the proper functioning of all cells and nervous tissue. It is extremely important because it helps control blood pressure and so reduces the risk of strokes, and also of kidney stones. Potassium is in all foods except oils, fats and sugars, but can be lost in the cooking water of vegetables, so use vegetable water for soups and stews.

Get advised daily amount from: an average-sized pizza with tomato purée, red peppers, broccoli, onions and garlic + 1 banana; a glass of tomato juice + 2 bananas + watercress, spinach and onion salad + 1 peach. Other good sources are root vegetables, green vegetables, tomato sauce, radishes and tropical fruits.

What is an ORAC?

Why is it that the French have less heart disease, Greek men live longer, Japanese women have less breast cancer and osteoporosis and don't even have a word for hot flushes? The riddle was solved by scientists in America. The US Department of Agriculture funds the Human Nutrition Research Centre on Ageing at Tufts University in Boston, where they've been studying antioxidants for some years. Researcher Dr Rob Prior and his colleagues decided to look at the antioxidant properties of whole foods rather than the individual vitamins and minerals they contain.

In their natural state, plants contain over 4,000 different antioxidant chemicals, which protect against many life-threatening conditions, such as heart disease, arterial damage, many forms of cancer and skin ageing – particularly wrinkles. The Tufts researchers discovered that the protective value could be measured – they referred to the units of measurement as Oxygen Radical Absorption Capacity units, or ORACs – and that the highest protection against all these diseases is achieved when the daily diet provides 5,000 ORACs. In the UK, we struggle to achieve a daily intake of 1,500 ORAC units, but nothing could be easier than boosting this to 5,000 and more.

So where do you find these miracle foods? At the greengrocer, the street market or, best of all, in your own Superfoods garden. They are simple, everyday, inexpensive fruits and vegetables. Colour is a good guide. The highest ORAC scores are found in deeply coloured produce – dark green, deep red, purple, blue, yellow and bright orange. Of course, vitamins and minerals are essential to life but it's the ORAC score that helps determine how long, how healthy and how free from disease and premature ageing that life is going to be.

The interaction between all the natural chemicals a plant contains produces this magical benefit, so you have to eat the foods – you can't get it from any pill. Remember, 5,000 is the optimum number of ORAC units to aim for, and here's the easiest way to get them.

Prunes
5,770 per 100g (3½oz) – 115 per cent of daily requirement
ORAC score: 10/10

Blueberries
2,400 per 100g (3½oz) – 48 per cent of daily requirement
ORAC score: 5/10

Curly kale
1,770 per 100g (3½oz) – 53 per cent of daily requirement from average 150g (5oz) portion
ORAC score: 5/10

Strawberries
1,540 per 100g (3½oz) – 46 per cent of daily requirement from average 150g (5oz) portion
ORAC score: 5/10

Spinach
1,260 per 100g (3½oz) – 30 per cent of daily requirement from average 120g (4¼oz) portion
ORAC score: 3/10

Brussels sprouts
980 per 100g (3½oz) – 29 per cent of daily requirement from average 150g (5oz) portion
ORAC score: 3/10

Plums
950 per 100g (3½oz) – 38 per cent of daily requirement from average 200g (7oz) portion
ORAC score: 4/10

Garlic
1,940 per 100g (3½oz) – 19 per cent of daily requirement from average 50g (2oz) portion
ORAC score: 2/10

Useful addresses

Harrod Horticultural
Pinbush Road
Lowestoft
Suffolk NR33 7NL
Tel 0845 402 5300
www.harrodhorticultural.com
This is a great company that has a large range of garden needs, including Sneerboer, the best tools in the world. Three Dutch brothers, Aad, Jaap and Frank Sneeboer, make gardening tools for the company founded by their grandfather in 1913. Using a coal fire, an anvil and a hammer, each tool is hand-forged, sharpened and fitted with a wooden handle.

Lakeland
Alexandra Buildings
Windermere
Cumbria LA23 1BQ
Tel 015394 88100
www.lakeland.co.uk
This is one of my favourite of all companies for superb quality, service and speedy delivery in UK and EU. Kitchen and garden stuff is all practical and great value for money.

Thompson & Morgan (UK) Ltd
www.thompson-morgan.com
Tel 0844 248 5383
One of the best selections of seeds including old varieties.

Soil Association
South Plaza
Marlborough Street
Bristol BS1 3NX
Tel 0117 314 5000
www.soilassociation.org
For all organic information, plants, seeds and products.

Jekka's Herb Farm
Rose Cottage
Shellards Lane
Alveston
Bristol BS35 3SY
Tel 01454 418878
www.jekkasherbfarm.com
Without doubt the best herb grower in Europe.

Seeds of Italy Ltd
A1 Phoenix Industrial Estate
Roslyn Crescent
Harrow HA1 2SP
Tel: 0208 427 5020
In the EC – www.seedsofitaly.com
In the USA – www.growitalian.com
For a surprising selection of all your favourite Italian vegetables and lots more besides.

Index

Acknowledgements

I could not have finished this book without the help of many people – particularly when I was suddenly taken into hospital with it only half written. I must thank Hervé Roncière, our photographer, who was immeasurably patient. I couldn't have done all the hard graft without our wonderful friend and gardener, Eddy Caudron-Willefert. Our fantastic neighbours, Mugette Confais and Claude Rimbault, have made life such fun here in France and have taught me the secrets of bottling, preserving, making pâté and putting corks in bottles of wine. Special mention, also, for Mme Dupin, our other neighbour who, in her eighties, would arrive with barrows of produce from her garden. We have happy memories of her dear husband Albert, who sadly died while I was writing this book.

Then there is Olfi, the hunting dog from the adjacent vegetable garden, seen here on the right, and his owners Jacques and Yvette Benon. He was there early each morning and wanted a bit of fuss, and they were an endless source of help, advice and local garden lore. Fred Masse, owner of the local second-hand and antique shop, found us props, old tools and containers and loaned some of his own things, all of which you will see in the photos.

This book has been a real joint effort with my wife Sally, or Céline as she is known here, and we both thank our wonderful butcher, fishmonger and all the people in our little town on Le Loir, who have made us so welcome in our exciting new adventure.

It goes without saying that I am hugely indebted to everyone at Cico Books – particularly Cindy Richards, Sally Powell and especially our editor, Gillian Haslam. I can't believe how understanding they were when one deadline after another went past while I was in hospital and then recuperating.

If you would like to keep up to date with Michael, access all his health advice, diets for losing or gaining weight, hundreds of health questions and natural answers, and get his monthly newsletters – all absolutely free – go to www.michaelvanstraten.com